William Pitt

I WILLIAM PITT IN 1805
Detail from the portrait by John Hoppner

William Pitt

JOHN W. DERRY

Had'st thou but lived, though stripp'd of power,
A watchman on the lonely tower,
Thy thrilling trump had roused the land,
When fraud or danger were at hand;
By thee, as by the beacon-light,
Our pilots had kept course aright;
As some proud column, though alone,
Thy strength had propp'd the tottering throne:
Now is the stately column broke,
The beacon-light is quench'd in smoke,
The trumpet's silver sound is still,
The warder silent on the hill!

Sir Walter Scott—*Marmion*

ARCO PUBLISHING COMPANY, Inc.
NEW YORK

First published 1963 *in the United States by*
ARCO PUBLISHING COMPANY, Inc.
480 Lexington Avenue, New York 17, N.Y.

© *John W. Derry, 1962*

Printed in Great Britain

Contents

Acknowledgment

The Author and Publishers wish to thank the following for permission to reproduce the illustrations appearing in this book:

Barclays Bank Ltd., for fig. 15.

The Trustees of the British Museum, for figs. 6, 9, 16–18 and 20.

The Fitzwilliam Museum, Cambridge, for fig. 14.

Dr. Katharine Fremantle, for fig. 21.

Leeds City Art Gallery, for fig. 10.

The National Portrait Gallery, for figs. 1, 3, 7, 8 and 19.

The Master and Fellows of Pembroke College, Cambridge, for fig. 4.

The Earl Stanhope, for figs. 2 and 11.

University Library, Cambridge, for fig. 5.

List of Illustrations

1 CHILDHOOD AND YOUTH
1759–1781

> I have been this morning with Lady Hester Pitt, and there is little William Pitt, not eight years old, and really the cleverest child I ever saw; and brought up so strictly and so proper in his behaviour, that, mark my words, that little boy will be a thorn in Charles's side as long as he lives.

VIEWED from the convenient distance of two hundred years, Lady Holland's words acquire a significance they did not possess when she used little William's conduct to contrast Lord Holland's affectionate indulgence with Chatham's no less tender, but more sober, discipline. Though Charles Fox's mother proved a wiser prophet than most parents, few could have anticipated that the rivalry between the fathers would be echoed and heightened in the antagonism of their sons. What is certain, is that the object of Lady Caroline's foreboding was an unusually gifted child: it is almost as if he was chosen and prepared in his cradle for an exceptionally testing, as well as an exalted, destiny.

He was born on 28 May 1759 at Hayes, near Bromley, in Kent, the fourth child and second son of William Pitt and Hester Grenville. A third son, James Charles, was born two years later and completed the family. Most of William's boyhood was spent at his birthplace, and at his father's estate of Burton Pynsent in Somerset, with occasional visits to Lyme Regis to enjoy the benefits of the sea air, and to indulge in the luxury of sea-bathing. His mother was the sister of Earl Temple and of George Grenville, whose unimaginative diligence did so much to provoke the quarrel with the American colonists. His father was Secretary of State, and the architect of a series of unparalleled victories in war. His proud boast to the Duke of Devonshire—'My Lord, I am sure I can save this country, and nobody else can'—had been redeemed in splendid fashion. The year of William's birth saw British fortunes at their peak in the struggle with France. Every morning Horace Walpole asked what victories had been won for fear of missing one. Boscawen and Hawke scattered the French fleets at Lagos and Quiberon; Wolfe's daring on the Heights of Abraham won Canada for King George; only Lord George Sackville's hesitancy at Minden—stigmatised by many as cowardice—marred the satisfaction which the British felt at the success which crowned their efforts in Europe, India, the New World, the Indies, and on the high seas. 'Diamond' Pitt would have rejoiced to know that his grandson had proved himself of tougher fibre than his milksop father, and, although the Prince of Wales described Pitt in sinister terms as 'the blackest of hearts', there seemed nothing to cloud the horizon when the fortunes of war so happily confirmed that God-given superiority which the English claimed as their birth-right. Arrogant, insular, and aggressive, they eagerly looked forward to the fruits of victory: new markets, expanding trade, handsome profits, and abundant wealth. Their sturdy individualism, their buoyant self-confidence and indomitable courage, their Protestant contempt for the superstitions of Europe and the East, their whig distaste for the absolutisms of France, Spain, and the Empire—all these flourished in the glowing exultation of unbroken triumph. When the accession of George III led to the fall of Pitt and Newcastle, little William was too young to sense the full magnitude of his father's humiliation, or the dissatisfaction with which many of his countrymen greeted the Peace of Paris, condemned as an over-generous concession to the ancient enemy. Not everyone shared the young King's opinion that the war was 'bloody and expensive'. On the contrary, it had been just and necessary, as well as glorious and profitable. The succulent phantoms of a dictated peace were preferred to the real gains of the Seven Years War, and City merchants wagged their heads in sage agreement with William Pitt's prophecy, that the peace had given the French the means of recovering their prodigious losses, and of becoming once more formidable at sea.

The King—immature, conscientious, inspired by the highest motives, and obsessed not with some plot to subvert the constitution but rather with his responsibilities as its principal defender—installed his 'dearest friend', his tutor, the Earl of Bute, in office. Feared as the agent of closet government, and denounced by prevalent gossip as the lover of the Queen-Mother, he was disliked as a Scot. Worst of all, he was

2 LADY HESTER PITT
*Detail from the portrait
by Thomas Hudson*

3 WILLIAM PITT THE ELDER,
FIRST EARL OF CHATHAM
*Detail from the portrait,
artist unknown, after
Richard Brompton*

4 WILLIAM PITT, AS A BOY OF SEVENTEEN
From a drawing by an unknown artist

incompetent, for he lacked the resilience to take political decisions. The great plan to rescue the constitution degenerated into tasteless farce, and, as the King's youthful ideals wilted in the harsh glare of politics, emotional development brought disillusionment, as well as deliverance from excessive reliance on his tutor. Within a year Bute had resigned, but the great myth of 'George—be King!' had already been born.

Out of office, Pitt turned his attention to his family. His second son soon showed promise, far in excess of his elder brother. He could hardly talk before he was given the nicknames 'Philosopher' and 'Counsellor', because of his precocious seriousness. Before he was three, his mother wrote of the 'fineness of William's mind' which enabled him to enjoy 'with the highest pleasure' what was 'above the reach of any other creature of his small age'. When his father was created Earl of Chatham in 1766, on forming his ill-starred second ministry, William was heard to say that he was glad he was not the eldest son, for he wanted to serve his country in the House of Commons, like Papa. In the same year, he was writing solemn letters in Latin to his father, and by the time he was eleven he had mastered the pompous and inflated manner, which passed for style with Chatham:

> From the weather we have had here I flatter myself that the sun shone on your expedition, and that the views were enough enlivened thereby to prevent the drowsy Morpheus from taking the opportunity of the heat to diffuse his poppies upon the eyes of the travellers.

On the same day (31 July 1770) he wrote to his brother, John, in a less stilted strain, complimenting him upon his Greek, and talking gaily of his white mare—'more of a species of an elephant than any other'—which could 'carry houses or castles on her back'. Two years later his tragedy, *Laurentius of Clarinium*, the story of a minister's fidelity during a regency crisis, was acted at family theatricals at Burton Pynsent, with the young author himself in the role (prophetically enough) of the faithful servant. But his performance was criticised because of his graceless deportment and stiff gestures. For all his intellectual brilliance, William was embarrassingly shy, and, possibly because he had little experience of social intercourse, he lacked ease and assurance in his dealings with people. Too often his clumsiness and tactlessness were mistaken for arrogance, and he sought to hide his feelings behind a veil of haughty reserve. He never thoroughly mastered these deficiencies throughout his long political career, and they contributed to his estrangement from Fox, Shelburne, and his cousin, William Wyndham Grenville, though in each case there were faults on both sides. But these failings were mere spots on the sun. William Hayley, the poet, met William at Lyme Regis in 1773, and spoke of him as 'a wonderful boy of fourteen, who eclipsed his brother in conversation'.

He was educated privately. Chatham, who dated the decline of the morals of English youth from the time Charles Fox was at Eton, had unhappy memories of his own schooldays. He told Shelburne that there was no boy who was not cowed for life by his experiences at Eton, and, if public schools were suitable for boys of a forward and turbulent disposition, he thought them disastrous where there was any gentleness. And William was not only gentle. He had been the victim of all the illnesses of boyhood—chills, and sickness, and indigestion—as well as afflicted with hereditary gout. His mother constantly worried about his delicate constitution, and his frequent bouts of ill-health. (On the eve of adolescence, he was still short and thin, and weighed only six stone.) This, added to his father's views on education, decided the matter. William stayed at home, with the Reverend Edward Wilson, of Pembroke Hall, Cambridge, as his tutor.

His enthusiasm for his lessons was unbounded. The difficulty was to check his ardour, to teach him to husband his resources and discipline his impatient thirst for knowledge. Often he would stand by Mr. Wilson, as he read, his remarks frequently lighting up a subject, and impressing it upon his teacher's memory. He seemed not to learn, but merely to recollect. Whilst receiving a thorough grounding in Latin, Greek, and Mathematics, from Wilson, he was also given instruction by his father, who took a keen interest in his son's progress. Whenever his health permitted, he liked to teach his children. He read a chapter of the Bible to them every day, and this habit gave William such a comprehensive knowledge of the Scriptures that, thirty years later, he surprised Bishop Tomline by spotting a passage from the Apocrypha, when discussing the Bishop's book on the Thirty Nine Articles. If Chatham was impressed by any piece of eloquence, or any passage of prose, he would pass it on to his son for his attention. He warmly recommended the study of the Greek historians. Even more important was the training he gave his son in public speaking. William was regularly set to read a book in a foreign language, aloud in English, pausing where he was not sure of the right word until it came, and in later life he attributed his readiness in debate to the drilling he had received at his father's hands. He was also required, daily, to recite passages from the great poets, Shakespeare and Milton being the favourite choices for this purpose. By the time he was fourteen, he was far in advance of most boys of his age, and it was thought proper to send him to the University. Wilson naturally took the opportunity to recommend his own college, telling his wife that he did not think he could have acted more prudently in the affair:

> Mr. Pitt is not the child his years bespeak him to be. He has now all the understanding of a man, and is, and will be, my steady friend through life. . . . He will go to Pembroke, not a weak boy to be made a property of, but to be admired as a prodigy; not to hear lectures, but to spread light. His parts are astonishing and universal. He will be fully qualified for a wrangler *before he goes*, and be an accomplished classick, mathematician, historian, and poet.

Chatham was unable to accompany his son on the journey to Cambridge: 'apprehensions of gout' made it too risky a business. But he wrote a characteristic letter to the Senior Tutor of Pembroke, apologising for his absence, and commenting on his son's prospects:

> An ingenuous mind and docility of temper will, I know, render him conformable to your Discipline, in all points. Too young for the irregularities of a man, I trust he will not, on the other hand, prove troublesome by the Puerile sallies of a Boy. Such as he is, I am happy to place him at Pembroke; and I need not say, how much of his Parents' Hearts goes along with him. . . .

On 8 October 1773 William Pitt, now a tall lank stripling, came into residence at Pembroke Hall.

But he had outgrown his strength. He fell ill almost at once, and Wilson stayed with him for several weeks. For two months he was confined to his rooms, charming all who attended him by his patience. Even when he had recovered sufficiently to go home for six months' convalescence, the journey from Cambridge to London took four days, because of his weakness. Chatham called in Dr. Addington, the family physician, who prescribed a regimen of port wine, early hours, and daily exercise on horseback. Pitt thrived on the cure, adhering to it long after his return to Cambridge in 1774. He threw off the ailments of his childhood in late adolescence, and until his strength flagged under the strain of the war with revolutionary France, he enjoyed good health.

At Cambridge he showed the same diligence and dazzling brilliance which had been so characteristic of his boyhood. He was now in the charge of the Reverend George Pretyman, whose primness obscured his ability. A close friendship sprang up between master and pupil, which eventually earned Pretyman the Bishopric of Lincoln, and the duty of becoming Pitt's biographer—a job which he bungled because of his timorous reverence for his old pupil. At Chatham's request, his son studied Thucydides and Polybius, and on his own initiative he attended lectures on Quintilian, Civil Law, and experimental philosophy. He took his degree by privilege in 1776, but remained in residence, worshipping in college chapel morning and evening, dining in hall unless indisposed, and spending most of the day in his tutor's company. Pretyman never knew him spend an idle day, or be late for any appointment. Pitt stuck rigorously to Addington's recommendation of early hours, finding that they made academic life 'agree perfectly'. His interest in mathematics was abiding. Shortly before leaving Cambridge, he told Pretyman that he hoped to find the leisure, and the opportunity, of reading Newton's *Principia* with him after the summer circuit. He admired Locke, Robertson, Hume, and Bolingbroke, but disliked the style of both Dr. Johnson and Edward Gibbon. He continued the practice of extemporaneous translation, earnestly comparing the set speeches in Thucydides, Livy, and Sallust, and noting down any striking expressions. In later life, opponents asserted that he valued the classics only as the source of quotations for his political speeches. After admission to his degree, he mixed rather more freely, and within a small circle of friends he was lively and popular, excelling in playful wit and quick repartee, an aspect of his character which few of his contemporaries appreciated. Improving health brought greater self-confidence, but there was never any irregularity in his conduct, and his lifelong continence inspired many taunts and gibes on the part of political enemies, who never tired of referring to the immaculate minister, who knew no woman.

Politics had always been his first love, and as he approached manhood boyish enthusiasm matured into an absorbing preoccupation.

The 'seventies were marked by great political strife, by bitter controversy and sour rivalry. Attempts made by various British governments to tax the American colonists had resulted in estrangement. Efforts to achieve some measure of conciliation failed, for it was impossible to disguise the decisive difference between the British and American points of view. Both sides became more uncompromising. The Americans reiterated their slogan of 'No taxation without representation', and resorted to acts of defiance. The British affirmed the sovereignty of Parliament, and replied with repressive and punitive legislation. The price of folly had now to be paid in blood and humiliation, as well as in gold and the shallow recantations of politicians. The shots fired by the embattled farmers had been heard round the world. Lord North, amiable, skilled in debate, prone to agonising fits of melancholy and inertia, dutifully carried out a policy which he distrusted, and remained in a situation which he loathed. Bound to his royal master by ties of gratitude and service, he stayed on while the Declaration of Independence and Saratoga confirmed what the Boston Tea Party and Lexington had begun, and as British inefficiency facilitated the success of American arms. Defeat sapped North's resolve, but, whilst the minister longed for a way out of the impasse, George III hardened his heart. The King was convinced that the future welfare of his dominions hinged on the outcome of the American War. Once the thirteen colonies were lost, Britain was doomed. She would fall a prey to the jealous nations of the Continent, who were unreconciled to their losses in the Seven Years War, and who saw in Britain's embarrassment their great opportunity. The King had no wish to preside over the disintegration of his empire: to do so would be to fail in his duty to God and man. In moments of depression, strange fantasies of abdication haunted his mind and he thought of Hanover and peace, but he shook himself out of these dismal moods to answer the call of an imperial destiny. The British people agreed with the King, until they were disillusioned by the length and expense of the conflict, and a mournful sequence of defeats. In the Commons, Gibbon and his colleagues, impressed but not convinced by the eloquence of Fox and Burke and the other opponents of the war, trooped submissively into the lobbies, consoling themselves with the thought that they were supporting 'with many a sincere and silent vote, the rights, though not, perhaps, the interest, of the mother-country'. To the end of his life George III thought the American War the most justifiable any country had ever waged, returning to it at times of mental stress, and fighting in unbalanced enthusiasm the battles of long ago.

During his years at Cambridge, William Pitt went up to London for the great debates, taking great care to hear his father speak on as many occasions as possible. But the long ascendancy of North only made Chatham seem more like a ghost from the distant past, a gaunt and haggard relic of a bygone era. His mental collapse during his second ministry, and his attempt to direct policy by remote control, had had catastrophic results, and his acceptance of a peerage had weakened his popularity. But as the blunders of the King and his ministers converted the dispute with the colonists into a struggle against the old enemy, Chatham's appeals for conciliation with the Americans, in order to wage war more effectively against the French, struck an answering chord in British hearts. Few questioned the last efforts of the hero to preserve for posterity the heritage he had done so much to win, and when, on 7 April 1778, he made his dying speech in the House of Lords, swathed in flannel, his voice scarcely more than a thin and barely audible croak, the American tragedy became more real, more tangible, more disturbing, than before. Chatham collapsed as he made his desperate plea for reconciliation, and he was carried home by his second son, and his son-in-law, Lord Mahon. On 11 May he died. Both Lords and Commons voted him a public funeral, together with a grant of £20,000 towards the payment of his debts, and an annuity of £4000 for his heirs. Only the King demurred, confessing that the compliment was 'rather an offensive measure to me personally'. On 9 June, Chatham was buried with great ceremony in Westminster Abbey, and William Pitt, chief mourner because of his elder brother's absence on active service, described the scene to his mother:

> I cannot let the servants return without letting you know that the sad solemnity has been celebrated so as to answer every important wish we could form on the subject. The Court did not honour us with their countenance, nor did they suffer the procession to be as magnificent as it ought; but it had notwithstanding everything essential to the great object, the attendance being most respectable, and the crowd of spectators immense. The Duke of Gloucester was in the Abbey. Lord Rockingham, the Duke of Northumberland, and all the minority in town were present. The pall-bearers were Sir G. Savile, Mr. Townshend, Dunning, and Burke. The eight assistant mourners were Lord Abingdon, Lord Cholmondeley,

5 PEMBROKE COLLEGE, CAMBRIDGE (THE ROOMS OCCUPIED BY WILLIAM PITT ARE THE FIRST-FLOOR ROOMS ON THE LEFT OF THE PICTURE)

6 DOWNING STREET IN THE EARLY NINETEENTH CENTURY
From a watercolour drawing by J. C. Buckler

7 WILLIAM PITT
*From the watercolour
by James Gillray*

8 CHARLES JAMES FOX
*From a contemporary chalk drawing
by an unknown artist*

Lord Harcourt, Lord Effingham, Lord Townshend, Lord Fortescue, Lord Shelburne, and Lord Camden. All our relations made their appearance. . . . I will not tell you what I felt on this occasion, to which no words are equal; but I know that you will have satisfaction in hearing that Lord Mahon as well as myself supported the trial perfectly well, and have not at all suffered from the fatigue. The procession did not separate until four o'clock. . . .

With an income of no more than £250–300 to look forward to, William had now to consider a career. As a student at Cambridge he had been attracted to the law, and, once the decision to read for the Bar had been made, the question arose of the purchase of chambers at Lincoln's Inn. The expense involved worried the young man:

> While I was in town I saw a set which are to be disposed of, and which have no other fault than being too dear and too good. At the same time I heard of none at an inferior price, which were not as much too bad. The whole expense of these will be eleven hundred pounds, which sounds to me a frightful sum. . . .

Fortunately, Earl Temple, Pitt's uncle, came to the rescue, lending the money required as an advance on his nephew's inheritance on attaining his majority, and the fledgling barrister now kept term at Lincoln's Inn. It was during this period that he had his famous encounter with Gibbon at a dinner-party given by Bland Burges. The historian had made a characteristic comment on the 'fashionable levities of political doctrine then prevalent', when he was interrupted by a deep voice from the other end of the table, questioning the accuracy of his statement. Gibbon turned on his youthful assailant, but he was compelled to withdraw his assertions, step by step, and, exasperated by this unusual change of fortune, left the party in a fit of pique. His host tried to prevail upon him to return, but Gibbon was adamant:

> that young gentleman, is, I have no doubt, extremely ingenious and agreeable, but I must acknowledge that his style of conversation is not exactly what I am accustomed to, so you must positively excuse me.

Pitt still followed debates in Parliament with critical interest: no sooner had he been introduced to Charles James Fox, than he was eagerly discussing how arguments, used in the debate which had just concluded, might have been met. Although he was called to the Bar

on 12 June 1780 and busy on the Western Circuit in the summer of
that year, he nevertheless looked towards Westminster with impatient
and ambitious eyes. He was determined to realise his boyhood dream
of speaking in the Commons, and in July 1779 he had confessed his
hopes to his mother. Writing from Cambridge, he had told her that
he had

> lately found very good reason to hope that the University may furnish me
> with a seat in Parliament, possibly at the General Election. It is a seat of all
> others most desirable, as being free from expense, perfectly independent,
> and I think in every respect extremely honourable . . . six candidates have
> declared already; but I assure you I shall not flatter myself with any
> vain hopes.

His caution was justified: Parliament was dissolved on 1 September
1780, and in the ensuing contest Pitt found himself bottom of the poll
at Cambridge. His youthful visions seemed shattered; he would have
to wait for some considerable time before he could enter politics. But
through the intervention of one of his University friends, the Duke of
Rutland, who mentioned his name to Sir James Lowther, he was
returned for the latter's pocket borough of Appleby, on the understanding that, in the event of any major difference of opinion between
Sir James and himself, he would vacate the seat.

He had suffered two more blows since his father's death. His sister,
Hester, who had married Lord Mahon in 1774, died in 1780, and later
in the same year news came that James Charles, the youngest of the
family, had died in the West Indies. Pitt was still young, and very
inexperienced, but he had known the chastening of bereavement three
times in three years. Because he had spent so much of his life in the
closed, intense atmosphere of books and learning, he underestimated
the difficulties of imposing his will on events—the intractable resilience
of human affairs, the unpredictable twists of political fortune. He had
no political influence, and few political connections. His only asset was
his name, and even its utility was dubious. Yet from the beginning he
fixed his gaze on the greatest offices, turning his attention to the gravest
and most controversial issues. With a sure hope that was the product
of his guarded upbringing, and strict, sheltered education, he did not
doubt that his hour would come. He had left the carefree days of youth
behind him now, and he was never to know again the unhurried

liberty of his years at Cambridge, when he could read avidly, talk incessantly, and ride and drink with his companions with a light heart, and a head intent on acquiring wider knowledge and a deeper understanding. The world of men was a more difficult, and less certain, conquest than the world of books, and in his private life he was never to know the refreshing peace which Fox found amidst the domestic happiness of St. Anne's Hill. Of the twenty-five years which remained to him, nineteen were spent in high office, during a period of international anarchy, and revolutionary social and political change. All his energies were to be devoted to meeting the problems bequeathed by one war, and created by another. He gave to politics and to government the same consuming and unflinching devotion which, in his boyhood, and youth, he had given to his studies. Yet his schemes of reform were, for the most part, foiled, and, despite all his greatness, there was a tragic irony about his career. The young reformer became the symbol of conservatism, the anti-Jacobin, the guardian of the old order; the man of peace was transformed by the merciless pressure of events into the Pilot who weathered the Storm; and the life which began to the accompaniment of the celebrations greeting Chatham's victories, closed in the shadow of Ulm and Austerlitz, when even Trafalgar's glory was tarnished by the memory of Nelson's death. There was, of course, much else besides frustration; in both war and peace real achievements were to be credited to Pitt's name; but when the raw and untried Member for Appleby took his seat in the House of Commons on 23 January 1781 he was setting out on a path which led to unremitting, and often unrewarded toil, as well as to the conventional acclamations of public fame, and the final consummation of a grave in Westminster Abbey. He was not yet twenty-two years of age.

2 IN POLITICS, 1781–1784

AT the beginning of 1781, Lord North and his colleagues seemed more securely established in office than ever. Not only had they been heartened by a successful general election, but Cornwallis's victories at Camden and Guildford Courthouse encouraged them to believe that the campaign in the Carolinas would reach a favourable—perhaps a decisive—conclusion. The King remained convinced that the policy which he had urged so vigorously upon his lethargic minister would be vindicated by events, and Lord George Germain's cheerful confidence in the enthusiastic devotion of countless American loyalists was unshaken. The British commanders in the revolted colonies did not share this bright optimism, but it was easy for men, who were far from the scene of the conflict, to ignore the problems facing Cornwallis as his weary army trudged on to Yorktown, imagining, as they did, that fair words at Westminster could miraculously assuage a situation already embittered by violence and intransigence on both sides. Whilst the ministers of the Crown clung to their illusions with all the blind devotion of doomed men, the whigs continued to denounce, not only the incompetence with which the war had been waged, but also the objects for which it was being fought.

Yet there was little unity within their ranks. The impression of a 'two-party' system, so easily given by the controversy over the American War, is false and deceptive. The average Member of Parliament staunchly refused to identify himself with any one party. Men still thought that there was a 'national' policy, which was obvious to all true patriots. Party was distrusted as factious, as the sinister attempt to impose the will of a minority upon the King. The government of the country was the King's business, and it was the duty of the Commons to support an administration which had the King's confidence, until the ministers had endangered the national interest by their mismanagement of public affairs. George III was a constitutional monarch, but as such he was the effective head of the executive. Men of goodwill, therefore, gave their approval to the government of the day, providing that it was not especially unpopular. There was little party organisation within the House of Commons, and less in the constituencies. Family alliances, personal friendships, local patriotisms, played as great a part as political conviction in moulding conduct. A great public issue might divide the House, but harmony would be restored, once the crisis had passed. An outstanding figure might build up a personal following, but his hold over his adherents was uncertain. In circumstances like these, parties were transient, but three broad classes were constant: the 'Court' party, or 'placemen', whose offices committed them to the government; the country gentlemen, who prided themselves on their independence, but who usually gave a fair hearing to any minister approved by the King; and the various groups of active politicians, contending for power, whose behaviour often appears wilful and inconsistent by modern 'party' standards. The whig opposition in 1781 illustrates this diversity. One section followed the Marquis of Rockingham, another the Duke of Portland. A small band of friends had gathered round the attractive, but unpredictable, Charles James Fox. Those who thought of themselves as disciples of Chatham acted together under the Earl of Shelburne. Personal animosities and mutual suspicions remained unabated, and although these rivalries could be obscured as long as there was an unjust war to inveigh against, they proved disastrous when the associated whig factions took office after the fall of North. But, whatever their faults, and however loose their organisation, the whigs constituted a genuine political opposition. Their distaste for the policy of coercion in America was sincere, and, in some cases, deeply felt; and, once the feud between Fox and Shelburne became irrevocable, the fusion of Foxites, Rockinghamites, and Cavendishes proved durable until shaken by the Regency Crisis and shattered by the French Revolution.

It was not surprising that William Pitt should attach himself to the Shelburne whigs, on his entry into the House of Commons. But, if this act can be interpreted as a gesture of filial devotion, his ostentatious independence showed him to be his father's son. He was loyal to Shelburne, but never subservient to him, and, like Chatham a generation earlier, he saw himself as a non-party man, a patriot above the crudities of faction, and the pettiness of party strife. It was possible, too, for Pitt and Fox to work together: they were, as yet, friendly rivals. Both opposed the American War; both advocated Parliamentary reform. But they were never close friends, despite Fox's characteristic generosity in proposing Pitt at Brooks's Club. Sharing several common interests, they had a mutual respect for each other's ability, but there was little intimacy in their relationship.

Pitt soon distinguished himself in debate, and he was promptly hailed as a worthy successor to his father. His fluent delivery, and clear, resonant voice, more than compensated for the angularity of his gestures. Burke called him 'the old block himself', and William Wilberforce thought him 'a ready made orator'—'I shall one day or other see him the first man in the country.' Pitt had every reason to be happy 'beyond measure' at the encouragement which had attended his first speech. Significantly, it had been made in support of Burke's motion calling for economic reform, on 26 February 1781. By carefully pruning the Civil List and other forms of expenditure and patronage, it was hoped to limit the influence of the Crown, which Pitt described as 'more to be dreaded because more secret in its attacks and more concealed in its operations than the power of the prerogative'. Such language endeared him to his colleagues, and when, on 12 June, he spoke in favour of Fox's motion for an immediate peace with the Americans, he attacked the administration with immense verve, denouncing the war as

> a most accursed, wicked, barbarous, cruel, unnatural, unjust, and diabolical war. It was conceived in injustice; it was nurtured and brought forth in folly; its footsteps are marked with blood, slaughter, persecution, and devastation; in truth everything which goes to constitute moral depravity and human turpitude are to be found in it. . . .

But mere eloquence, however much it redounded to the credit of a young and inexperienced Member, did not shake the stubborn majority, who remained faithful to North. Hopes of victory still flourished, vain and fatuous, but undeniably seductive. They were soon cruelly disappointed.

For the situation resumed its customary gravity. Holland had joined France and Spain in formidable alliance against Great Britain; in the Baltic the Armed Neutrality threatened British interests, and frustrated British policy; in India, Hyder Ali swept through the Carnatic; the garrison of Gibraltar, pugnaciously defiant under General Eliott, was still besieged. Even the campaign which had begun so promisingly ended in tragedy and gloom. A French, not a British, fleet controlled Chesapeake Bay, and Yorktown became a trap, not a refuge. On 19 October 1781 the exhausted British army surrendered, the news reaching London on 25 November. 'Oh God! It's all over!' exclaimed North, on hearing of the catastrophe. He had now little doubt that peace with the rebels was imperative. But although his minister had no faith in further attempts to compel the Americans to return to their allegiance, George III was resolute in the face of adversity, and, as on former occasions, North was kept in office by the relentless will of his master. Throughout the winter the government's majority dwindled until it had shrunk to ten on a motion of censure, on 8 March 1782. Even George III realised how serious the plight of the ministry had become. He opened negotiations with the detested Rockinghamites, Thurlow, the Lord Chancellor, acting as intermediary. The King hoped that Rockingham and his associates would join North in a 'broad-bottom' ministry, but the Marquis had no wish to prolong the existing government under a new guise. He insisted that there should be no veto on the recognition of the independence of the United States, and demanded freedom to introduce a programme of economic reform. He called for the exclusion from the ministry of all 'who had been considered as obnoxious ministers, or . . . who were deemed as belonging to a sort of secret system'. This was nothing less than an ultimatum to the King. Such conditions were unacceptable, for George III was determined to retain his constitutional right to choose his ministers. Meanwhile, North pleaded for his release, and on 20 March he was finally permitted to resign, the King wryly commenting, 'Remember, my Lord, it is you who desert me, not I you.' The late minister announced his deliverance to a House which had assembled in expectation of a lengthy debate, and, as the Members waited for their carriages on an evening darkened by falling snow, he cheerfully greeted them, as he clambered into his coach—'Good night, gentlemen. You see what it is to be in the secret.' With his habitual amiability, North bade farewell to the cares of power: had he had his own way his good-byes would have been said years earlier, and no one, least of all North himself, imagined that in just over a year he would be back in office, with Fox, his most outspoken opponent, as his colleague.

But, though he had lost the minister whom he had forcibly retained in office for eleven years, the King did not submit to the whigs without a struggle. He tried to lure Shelburne into abandoning his friends, but when the Earl indicated that Rockingham must head any new ministry, George acquiesced. Rockingham became First Lord of the Treasury, with Shelburne and Fox as his Secretaries of State. William Pitt had no part in the ministry. Shelburne pressed his claims, but his youth was thought too great a handicap. Rockingham toyed with the idea of offering him the Vice-Treasurership of Ireland—a lucrative post, well suited to a promising and indigent young man—but Pitt had no desire to commit himself to one party. However ambitious, he was determined to preserve his independence. He had not expected a post, and had gone so far as to say that he would never accept 'a subordinate situation'. Pitt regretted this rash statement, almost as soon as the words were out of his mouth. Yet, although ill-advised, he had not spoken on the spur of the moment. His resolution was well thought over. Perhaps he sensed the insecurity haunting the Rockingham administration; the suspicions entertained of Shelburne; the hostile feelings which prevented Fox and Shelburne from working together in a friendly spirit. Pitt knew how easily the ministry might dissolve, how tenuous was the unity which hung on Rockingham's frail life. He had made his mark in the Commons: other offers would come in good time, perhaps all the more generous as a result of his haughty refusal. He had done no more than raise his price. It was wiser to wait, to allow the situation to develop before taking any decisive step, rather than to risk being caught up in the inner rivalries of the new ministry. And, at this time, Pitt was happy as an independent Member of Parliament. He enjoyed his leisure in the company of friends he had made at Cambridge, some of whom introduced him to a wider circle of acquaintances. At Goostree's he met other men with similar interests, and his wit and conversation made him a popular companion. But, despite his membership of Brooks's, he scrupulously avoided the gaming table. After tasting the 'increasing fascination' of games of chance, he 'soon . . . abandoned them forever'.

The Rockingham ministry was committed to peace with America, but Fox and Shelburne were in violent disagreement as to whether recognition of the independence of the United States should precede negotiations, or be dependent on their outcome. Shelburne was prepared to grant political independence to the thirteen colonies, but he appreciated the advantages to both Britain and America of retaining economic links, perhaps of sharing a common foreign policy. He sought a free partnership, which would prevent further estrangement. In order to win American goodwill, he was ready to be generous in drawing the frontiers of the new State. But all this was incomprehensible to the rest of the Cabinet. Nor was the situation made any easier by Rockingham's weakness as a leader. Although he was acceptable to the various groups which made up the whig party, Rockingham was a reticent personality, a feeble, almost an inaudible, speaker, and a wholly unoriginal thinker, who depended for his ideas on Edmund Burke. He was incapable of persuading Shelburne and Fox to collaborate effectively.

Shelburne—intelligent, perceptive, sympathetic to new ideas, and fond of the company of intellectuals—was distrusted by his political associates, as well as by his avowed enemies. His ambiguities in debate, his subtleties in negotiation, his notorious ability to qualify and refine meanings which were plain enough to everybody else, made him suspect. Most sinister of all was the fact that he was favourably regarded by the King. The gibe of the 'Jesuit of Berkeley Square' stuck, and, for all his undoubted gifts, Shelburne remains one of the most mysterious of eighteenth-century politicians. He never played as great a part in public life as a man of his intellectual stature ought to have done. Like many astute politicians with keen, inquiring minds, he could not convince colleagues of his sincerity. He failed, not because he lacked insight into the problems of the day, but because of his unsatisfactory relationships with other men in politics. The qualities which impress posterity do not always commend a man to his contemporaries, and the boldness and ingenuity, which so often give Shelburne's conceptions a startling modernity, stirred the darkest prejudices in the minds of those whose immediate reaction was that he was too clever by half.

Almost his every action displeased somebody. His conviction that independence for the Americans should form part of a general peace settlement made him agreeable to the King, but it brought him into direct conflict with Fox, who conveniently forgot that only Shelburne's powers of persuasion had reconciled George III to the necessity of recognising the United States at all. Fox claimed that foreign affairs lay within his department. Shelburne retorted that colonial matters fell within his sphere, and that he was therefore directly concerned with the settlement of the claims of the colonists. Each regarded the other with mounting distrust and undisguised hostility, and there could be no greater contrast than that between the subtle, scheming, highly sophisticated Shelburne, and the impetuous, emotional, uninhibited Fox.

Charles James Fox was the darling of whig society. Ten years older than William Pitt, he was the second son of Henry Fox, Chatham's old rival, who had been raised to the peerage as Lord Holland for his part in securing a majority in the Commons for the Peace of Paris. Charles Fox had been hopelessly spoilt by his fulsomely affectionate father, who had indulged every childish whim, as well as introducing his son early in life to the pleasures of the gaming table and race-course. Throughout his life, Fox flaunted his loose morals with the thoughtlessness of a boy. As a youth he had complained that Nice was a dull place: there were no whores. The capricious element in his personality was evident throughout his political career. Entering politics in 1768 as one of the most promising of the King's Friends, he had held office under North. But he proved a difficult colleague to control (he was never amenable to discipline) and in 1774 he was finally dismissed with little ceremony, and less regret. He had already made a name as a debater, and during the 'seventies he drew closer to the Rockinghamites, chiefly because of their opposition to the American War. But he was never a full member of the group, always remaining something of a freelance. His indiscretions were notorious, but no matter how often he infuriated companions, his tearful pleas for forgiveness soon restored him to favour. His language in debate was often violent, but he bore no grudges. His warm-hearted friendship, his charm, and his generosity were irresistible, but he was also ambitious, ruthless, and impatient of any obstacle in his path: the last was his undoing more than once. He was the self-conscious foe of 'the influence of the Crown' and his demands for a greater degree of Cabinet responsibility offended the King. A friend to Parliamentary reform, he was devoted to what he considered the cause of liberty, but, although he possessed insight and imagination in abundance, he lacked stamina. During his brief spells in office, he proved that he could master the intricacies of business, but his instability was deeply rooted, and, despite the legendary devotion which he has inspired, he was principally responsible for the futility of his career. Throughout the Rockingham ministry, he and Shelburne kept a wary eye on each other: within a few months their antagonism provoked a major political crisis, which exercised a decisive influence on the career of William Pitt.

In the closing months of war fortune favoured British arms. Rodney's defeat of de Grasse, and the relief of Gibraltar, enabled the government to open negotiations from a more advantageous position, whilst legislative independence did something to ease the troubled situation in Ireland. During the months immediately after the fall of North, Pitt played a leading part in supporting motions calling for Parliamentary reform. He was sufficiently interested to attend a meeting on 18 May 1782 at the Thatched House Tavern, under the auspices of the Society for Promoting Constitutional Information—an incident which was to be cited by the defence during the trial of John Frost for sedition in 1793. But Pitt never lost sight of the practical problems involved in any proposed scheme of reform, or of the strength of the opposition which would have to be faced. He saw himself not as creating a new constitution but as carefully refurbishing the existing machinery of representation and government, and he was content to accept the basic structure, whilst attempting to improve its efficiency. His speech of 7 May 1782, calling for the appointment of a committee of inquiry into the most prudent method of securing a 'moderate and substantial reform', admirably sums up his approach to the subject:

> It is of the essence of the constitution that the people should have a share in the government by the means of representation; and its excellence and permanency is calculated to consist in this representation, having been designed to be equal, easy, practicable, and complete. When it ceases to be so; when the representative ceases to have connection with the constituent, and is either dependent on the Crown or the aristocracy, there is a defect in the frame of representation, and it is not innovation but recovery of the constitution, to repair it.

But, though his speech was well received, Pitt's motion was rejected by 161 votes to 141.

The Rockingham ministry soon foundered, the victim of the inter-necine feuds which had divided its most gifted members, with its objectives of peace and reform still unattained. Rockingham had never been robust, and when he was carried off by influenza on 1 July 1782 the question arose—who would succeed him as first minister? Even whilst he lay dying, speculation had been widespread. When the King asked Shelburne to take over as First Lord of the Treasury, Fox and his friends were furious. Fox had bitterly resented Shelburne's intervention in the peace talks at Paris, and he was determined not to serve under him. He suggested that Portland should succeed, as head of the ministry, the two Secretaries of State remaining in their situations. Fox also claimed that the Cabinet had the right to choose the head of a ministry, and he did not disguise his conviction that the monarch should ratify the choice made by the ministers. This went far beyond the conventions recognised in the formation of ministries, and Shelburne lamented that such proceedings would reduce George III to the level of a King of the Mahrattas, 'who had nothing of sovereignty but the name'. The constitution would be no more. When George III refused to submit to their demands, Fox, Portland, and their friends resigned. They hoped to make it impossible for Shelburne to stay in office, but they had miscalculated badly. The King was never more dangerous than when he sensed any attempt to impose a ministry upon him, and he was well within his rights when he insisted on a free and unfettered choice of ministers. He and Shelburne resolved to bring in new men to strengthen the ministry, and, despite his lack of adminis-trative experience, Pitt was offered the Chancellorship of the Exchequer. His proud determination to refuse any minor post had borne spectacular results.

Shelburne had a high opinion of Pitt's ability, but his motives in offering him the Chancellorship were mixed. Though he considered himself a Chathamite, he did not allow sentiment to dictate policy, and with Fox, Burke, and Sheridan in opposition, the government needed a capable and persuasive spokesman in the Commons. Pitt had distin-guished himself in debate, and his refusal to serve as a junior minister under Rockingham had impressed his 'independence' on the House. Now his accession to the ministry would emphasise its patriotic

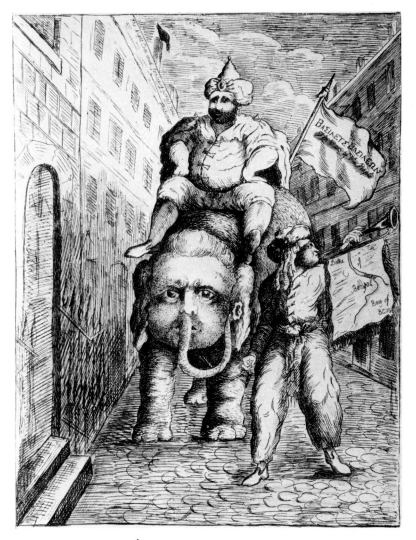

9   CARLO KHAN'S TRIUMPHAL ENTRY INTO LEADENHALL STREET
From a caricature by James Sayers, 1783

10 WILLIAM PITT
*From the portrait by
Gainsborough Dupont*

11 WILLIAM PITT AS A YOUNG MAN
From a sketch by J. S. Copley

character, while exposing Fox's error in destroying an administration over what seemed a matter of personal caprice. The majority of those who understood the issues at stake thought Fox a dangerous innovator. He had anticipated the speedy fall of Shelburne, and the immediate return of his friends and himself to office, but, now that Pitt had accepted the Chancellorship of the Exchequer, it was evident that Shelburne intended to stay and fight. Perhaps Fox ruefully wondered whether his differences with Shelburne had, after all, been insuperable: it is by no means certain that he would have been outvoted on every issue within the Cabinet. But, whatever the rights and wrongs of Fox's resignation, neither of the whig factions was strong enough to continue in office alone. Shelburne could either make up his quarrel with Fox, or come to an understanding with North, in order to obtain a comfortable majority in the Commons. And precisely the same choice lay before Fox.

For Pitt—young, ambitious, and fully aware of his own ability—Shelburne's offer was tempting; there was no reason for him to feel any loyalty to the Foxite whigs, who had precipitated the crisis by leaving the government. Yet he has been criticised for preferring Shelburne to Fox at this stage, and his entry into office has been denounced as the decisive step which made the dream-world alliance of Fox and Pitt an impossibility. But Pitt was bound to Fox by no political ties. Despite the similarity of their views on the American War and Parliamentary reform, Pitt agreed with George III and Shelburne on the issue over which Fox had resigned—the alleged right of the Cabinet to impose the head of an administration on the King. Throughout his career, he respected the King's convictions—on several occasions at some cost to himself—and he was content to work within accepted conventions. Unlike Fox, he introduced no novelties in constitutional doctrine, and his decision to join the Shelburne administration was consistent with his conservative approach to constitutional problems. He knew that the King looked towards him to play his part in saving the country from Mr. Fox, but his negotiations with Shelburne had been cautious, and his conversations with Fox on 2 July had been guarded and discreet. Fox had hinted that the death of Rockingham might lead to a restoration of the King's personal rule, and had warned Pitt, 'They look to *you*—without you they cannot succeed.' Pitt had replied that if they depended on him, they would find themselves mistaken. Fox was not satisfied that this meant a refusal to participate in any ministry with Shelburne at its head, but Pitt's behaviour becomes less sinister when it is remembered that he did not share Fox's opinion that Shelburne would revive the state of things which had existed under North. By dividing the fragile whig alliance, Fox had strengthened, not weakened, the King's hand, and several of his colleagues, including Richmond and Keppel, thought that he would have been wiser to have stayed on under Shelburne, until the new ministry had had the opportunity of proving itself.

Some support for this point of view can be deduced from Shelburne's own preference for a reconciliation with Fox, rather than an understanding with North. Pitt, who was steadfastly opposed to any compromise with North, acted as mediator, but negotiations ran into difficulties at once, Fox demanding Shelburne's resignation as First Lord of the Treasury. He was prepared to share the Secretaryships with him, as before, but he still insisted that Portland should be the nominal head of the ministry. Pitt's reply was succinct and conclusive: 'I have not come here to betray Lord Shelburne.' Fox had lost the opportunity to undo the harm inflicted on the whig party by his resignation, and his refusal to admit that he had been mistaken made it impossible for him to make his peace with the minister in a dignified and honourable fashion. The problem of obtaining a majority in the Commons was to be settled otherwise.

For Shelburne had missed the chance of coming to some agreement with North. George North and William Eden had brought about a reconciliation between Fox and the amiable victim of his most violent invective during the American War. In the Commons the coalition would be irresistible: not only was it superior in numbers to every other combination, but every notable debater, with the exception of Pitt himself, was ranged within its ranks. North's wit, Fox's brilliance, Burke's eloquence, and Sheridan's sparkling repartee, would all serve the same cause. But the programme of the coalition was not that of the Rockingham ministry. Nothing more was to be done in the way of economic reform, and (less surprisingly) everyone was to be at liberty to follow his own opinion on Parliamentary reform. In return, North consented to the control and direction of policy by the Cabinet: there was to be no repetition of that government by departments with which he was so familiar, and which he now condemned as a 'very bad system'.

For Fox the prospect was encouraging. He would take up his old post as Secretary of State, with North as his colleague. A long, secure tenure of power seemed inevitable, and this alone made the accommodation worth while. It was convenient to allow old quarrels to fade into oblivion, and to look forward to the humiliation of the King and Shelburne. Yet Fox was doing what Pitt has often been condemned for doing—seeking power first, trusting that, in due course, he would use it well.

The allies did not wait for long before demonstrating their new unity in action. On 30 November the provisional peace treaty with America had been signed, but confirmation of its terms depended on the settlement with France, Spain, and Holland. Despite difficulties within the Cabinet, the preliminaries of peace with the Continental powers were signed on 20 January. The terms were much more favourable to Britain than had at one time seemed likely. Tobago, St. Lucia, Miquelon, St. Pierre, Senegal, Goree, and her stations in India were returned to France; Florida and Minorca went to Spain; Trincomalee to the Dutch. Britain retained Dominica, St. Vincent, Grenada, St. Kitts, Nevis, and Montserrat, as well as her conquest of the Bahamas, and the courageously defended fortress of Gibraltar. But these terms were badly received in Parliament, and the government soon became involved in difficulties. When the ministry was defeated by sixteen votes in a division on the peace in the Commons, on 17 February 1783, Pitt thought the adverse vote decisive, but Shelburne would not admit defeat. He had been victorious in the Lords, and the majority against him in the Commons had been small. But when the government was defeated by seventeen votes on 21 February, after a debate on a set of resolutions criticising the peace, Shelburne was left with no alternative but resignation. On 24 February 1783 he surrendered the seals of office.

The other members of the Cabinet did not follow him immediately, and for a time it was hoped that the ministry would be able to carry on under another leader. But who could take over the leadership? Would Fox seek a reconciliation with those of his late colleagues who had remained in office, content now that he had driven Shelburne from power? Meanwhile, the King sought to outwit the coalition. He attempted to persuade North to desert his new associates, but, with his long and weary experience of conditions of service, North refused to enter a government without his companions. The King pressed Pitt to succeed Shelburne: the young minister was faced with a difficult decision: the highest office was now within his grasp, but were the auspices favourable? For several days he thought the matter over, changing his mind frequently, and seeing new obstacles in his way whenever he thought he had made up his mind. Eventually, he decided that the moment was inopportune, and busied himself with his duties as Chancellor of the Exchequer.

It was proving embarrassingly difficult to provide the country with a new and stable ministry. Portland and North had had differences of opinion over the allocation of Cabinet posts, and towards the end of March the King made a second approach to Pitt, but when it became known that the leaders of the opposition had made up their quarrel, he again declined to accept the first place in a new administration. Dundas confessed his bewilderment to his brother—'How all this anarchy is to end God only knows'—and the King told Pitt that he was much hurt

> to find you are determined to decline at an hour when those who have any regard for the Constitution as established by law ought to stand forth against the most daring and unprincipled faction that the annals of this kingdom ever produced.

But not even George III could resist much longer. The long delay in appointing a new administration had been criticised in the Commons, and on 31 March Pitt announced his resignation from the Exchequer. The King saw with horror that he would have to submit to the dreaded coalition, which was all the more hateful because it united his late minister and his most objectionable opponent. On 2 April the new ministers kissed hands, but it was noted that the King 'turned back his ears and eyes just like a horse at Astley's when the tailor he had determined to throw was getting on him'. Portland headed the ministry as First Lord of the Treasury; Fox and North became Secretaries of State; Lord John Cavendish succeeded Pitt as Chancellor of the Exchequer. But, even in their hour of triumph, one of the whigs warned that 'unless a real good government is the consequence of this junction, nothing can justify it to the public'. Events soon bore out Fitzpatrick's wisdom. Despite his capitulation, the King was on the look-out for an opportunity to rid himself of the loathsome ministry, and his attitude played as great a part in the discomfiture of the coalition as public feeling. Although George III did not indulge in intrigues against his new ministers at once, he made no attempt to disguise his feelings.

During the early months of the Fox-North administration, Pitt was content to lead the life of a private Member. He had affirmed, when announcing his resignation, that he was unconnected with any party, and that he would act with whichever side he thought right: he had no desire to identify himself too closely with Shelburne, or with any other group in politics. He had made his way by remaining independent, and, loyal as he had been to Shelburne during the abortive negotiations with Fox, he did not wish to imperil his prospects by relying on the distrusted and vanquished peer. It was essential for him to retain his freedom of action: circumstances could change so easily. Meanwhile he enjoyed the respite from high office, and in the summer of 1783 he spent much time with friends. Few Members of Parliament would have recognised the sober Chancellor in the practical joker whose boyish pranks enlivened Wilberforce's villa at Wimbledon. But he did not forget his duties in the House. On 7 May he introduced three resolutions on Parliamentary reform. The first pledged the House to take stricter measures for the prevention of bribery and corruption; the second called for the disenfranchisement of any borough whose electors were guilty of gross corruption; the third suggested an increase in the number of Members for London and the counties—a reform advocated by Chatham, who had shared the conventional eighteenth-century belief that the knights of the shire were the most honest and upright section of the legislature. Though Fox spoke on behalf of the resolutions, they were rejected by 293 votes to 149 in a House which forgot all other quarrels in the defence of its own privileges. But Pitt did not limit his attention to Parliamentary reform. In June he introduced a Bill for the reform of abuses in administration, by which he hoped to save £40,000 a year; but, after the Commons had approved the proposals without a division, they were thrown out by the Lords. Pitt was not downhearted, however. The reverse on Parliamentary reform had been much more complete than he had expected, but he did not think the discussion useless.

On 10 July, Pitt's brother, the Earl of Chatham, married Miss Mary Elizabeth Townshend, the daughter of Lord Sydney, and shortly after their honeymoon the couple entertained Pitt at Hayes. Always an affectionate and dutiful son, he visited his mother at Burton Pynsent, as well as spending some time at Stowe and Brighton. In September he went to France with his friends William Wilberforce and Edward Eliot, staying abroad until 24 October. It was on this trip that he met Talleyrand, as well as reminding the Abbé de Lageard, when the latter criticised Fox's morals, that he had never been 'under the wand of the magician'. Pitt prophesied that the royal prerogative and the authority of the House of Lords would be the first parts of the British constitution to perish, and shrewdly commented that, if the French had little political liberty, they enjoyed a greater degree of civil liberty than was commonly supposed. He was also the innocent cause of hysterical scenes in that most emotional of households—the Necker family. Madame Necker had the bright idea of marrying off her daughter, Germaine, to the young Englishman, but she neglected to inform the object of her calculations exactly what she had in mind for him. In fact, Pitt was no more eager to marry the future Madame de Staël than she was willing to accede to her mother's plans: the thought of leaving her father made her ill, and she did not want to live in England. A year later she was rebuked by her fond parent for her short-sightedness in blighting such a promising scheme: any suggestion that Pitt was not attracted to her daughter was beyond Madame Necker's comprehension. Happily he returned home without falling a victim to these continental marriage projects. He never went abroad again. For the rest of his life the cares of State and the international situation made it impossible for him to renew his acquaintance with the delights of a continental holiday.

He was soon immersed in another crisis. The King had never forgiven Fox and North for imposing themselves upon him, and he submitted to them with morose resentment. But before the coalition could be challenged with any hope of success some controversy was required which would appeal to outraged morality as well as to self-interest. At first, George III had thought of using the Prince of Wales's debts as a pretext for dismissing his ministers. Wisely, he listened to advice and bided his time. On 18 November, Fox introduced his India Bill.

It was certainly necessary to reform the administration of British India, and to control more effectively the affairs of the East India Company. North's Regulating Act of 1773 had given Parliament the right to supervise all matters of high policy, but this was shown to be defective in 1782, when the Company's Court of Proprietors reversed the decision of the Court of Directors to recall the Governor-General. Despite Hastings's great services during a period of exceptional difficulty, many disapproved of his willingness to use 'Oriental' methods in governing an eastern country. The very distinction with which he carried out his duties inspired envy amongst other employees of the Company, who deplored the presents the Governor received from ruling Princes only because they wanted a greater share of such benefits for themselves. Philip Francis bore Hastings an intense and withering grudge, and he spread tales of his rapacity with malicious enthusiasm. Burke and Fox responded in another fashion. The Irishman's imagination was stirred by the tragedy of an ancient civilisation exposed to the assaults of ruthless profiteers: government must be in the interests of the governed, not a mere device for private gain. Power implied responsibility. Fox, too, was convinced that the Company must be more efficiently regulated, and there can be no doubt of his sincerity in seeking to reform the administration of India. But, although he was aware of the dangers of meddling in the affairs of the East India Company, he did not take sufficient care to win over the Directors and shareholders, who did not feel his generous concern for the welfare of the Indians. The merits of his proposals were soon obscured by the controversy over the sanctity of charters and the control of patronage.

Fox proposed the creation of a Board of Seven Commissioners, with the power to appoint and dismiss those who held office in India. The names of the Commissioners were to be decided when the Bill was in Committee, and their authority was to last for four years, regardless of any changes in government. At the beginning of every session the India Board's accounts were to be laid before Parliament, whilst a council of eight would supervise the commercial activities of the Company. These proposals provoked a storm of abuse and misrepresentation. Many Members of Parliament had a personal interest in the East India Company, and they were fearful for their rights under its charter: these were more important than any high-flown talk about the rights of the natives, or the responsibilities of government. By making the Board immune from the vicissitudes of English politics, Fox had laid himself open to the accusation that he was seeking to exploit the Company's patronage as a security against future political defeat. His critics ignored the need for greater continuity in the management of Indian affairs, and denounced his measures as inspired by 'ambition, rapacity, and confiscation'. The Directors of the Company embarked on a campaign, with the slogan 'Our property and charter are invaded, look to your own.' Fox admitted that the Bill encroached on the rights granted in the original charter, but he defended his action on the grounds that a charter was a trust bestowed in return for a benefit, and that legislative interference was necessary in order to guarantee good government. This did not conciliate his opponents, who felt that their own privileges were threatened, and rash statements, such as the Attorney-General's description of a charter as 'only a skin of parchment with a seal of wax at the end of it', did not improve matters. The knowledge that Edmund Burke was the author of the Bill aroused more sinister suspicions. Controversy raged, not over the Bill's value in improving the government of India, but over Fox's alleged appropriation of patronage. Pitt made this the mainspring of his attack in an unfair but telling speech, and in the Press Fox was caricatured as 'Carlo Khan', entering Leadenhall Street in triumph, on an elephant with a pronounced facial resemblance to Lord North.

George III realised that this was the issue he had been waiting for. He would now be able to pose as the champion of public morality and good faith, besides satisfying his desire for revenge. But, like many of his subjects, he was sincerely apprehensive about any attack on charter rights, and Thurlow and Lord Temple had played on his fears, warning him that the Bill would deprive him of half of his power for the rest of his reign. He needed little persuasion. He was more than willing to play his part. But two questions remained: how could he exercise his influence in the most effective manner? and who would lead a new ministry, should Fox and North be dismissed? In the Commons the coalition stood firm, amidst all the fury of debate, the Bill being passed by 208 votes to 102 on 8 December. The second reading in the Lords was fixed for 15 December. On the 11th, Temple had a private interview with the King. He left with a letter, stating that His Majesty

> allowed Earl Temple to say that whoever voted for the India Bill was not only not his friend, but would be considered by him as an enemy; and if these words were not strong enough, Earl Temple might use whatever words he might deem stronger, and more to the purpose.

Meanwhile, Dundas renewed his efforts to convince Pitt that a new ministry stood a good chance of survival, and he was now armed with the latest researches of Robinson, the King's experienced electoral agent. On 15 December he and Pitt held a conference. There were indications that some Members were wavering in their loyalty to North, and that the India Bill had precipitated a controversy on which Fox could be fought with a real hope of success. Pitt gave way, promising to accept the Treasury if Fox and North were discharged. On 17 December the India Bill was defeated in the Lords by 95 votes to 76: Temple had made good use of the King's letter. On the same day, Fox and North condemned his conduct as a high crime and misdemeanour, and when Pitt intervened in the debate Fox rebuked him in a speech which made pointed reference to 'boys without judgment, without experience of the sentiments suggested by a knowledge of the world'.

Temple's tactics revived all the old suspicions about closet government, and the King's intervention in the Lords debate was of doubtful validity. But he gained no easy victory. The ministers reaffirmed their determination to reform the government of India, and stigmatised as a public enemy anyone who should advise the King to interpose his influence between them and their objective. George III waited impatiently for Fox and North to resign: he had anticipated surrender, not defiance. Late on the night of 18 December, when he could bear neither the suspense nor the disappointment any longer, he sent messages to the chief ministers, commanding them to deliver up their seals of office. On the next day, Temple was installed as Secretary of State.

But the struggle for power was only beginning. The coalitionists were still in a substantial majority in the Commons, and they felt their humiliation with unconcealed bitterness. Their schemes of reform, and their prospects of power, had both been thwarted. They claimed—with some justice—that they had been the victims of a dastardly manœuvre. The King, on the other hand, thought that he had done no more than repay his adversaries in their own coin. They had conspired against a minister who had possessed his confidence and had imposed their will upon their sovereign, in defiance of his recognised right to choose his own ministers. The Lords and Commons were constitutionally required to give every minister the chance of proving himself: they had not done so, when hounding Shelburne out of office by a low conspiracy. The collusion with Temple was no worse than the Fox-North coalition. For the King to procure the defeat of a ministry

which he abhorred, and which had sought to undermine the prerogative of the Crown in order to maintain a faction in office, was a just
response to Parliamentary intrigue. Fox was well in advance of his
time, when he asserted that the Commons had long been the real agent
of government, with the right to force a ministry upon the King; and
although he conceded that the King's veto on legislation was an
acceptable method by which a monarch could indicate his lack of
confidence in a ministry, he deprived this of significance by insisting
that it should be employed only after the ministers had been consulted.
It is not surprising that George III saw Fox and his colleagues as
'desperate men', contriving the ruin of 'the most perfect of all human
formations—the British Constitution'. They intended to take from
him 'the only two remaining privileges of the Crown'—the right to
veto legislation, and the liberty to select ministers. If these were
infringed, he confessed to Pitt in February 1784, 'I cannot but feel, as
far as regards my person, that I can be no longer of any utility to this
country, nor can with honour continue in this island.'

Pitt had accepted a responsibility which he had declined earlier in
the year, because the powerful influence and vast resources of the
East India Company would be thrown into the fray against the late
ministers. The King and the Company made a formidable combination, and the knowledge that, if he could hold on long enough,
preparations would be made to ensure victory in a general election
turned the scales in bringing him to a decision. It was encouraging to
recall that no government had lost a general election for over forty
years. Although Pitt probably knew of Temple's ruse in advance, he
was not directly involved in the fall of his predecessors, and he did not
concern himself with the means by which Fox had been driven from
office. He was no doctrinaire, and sound finance meant more to him
than irreproachable whig doctrine. Nor was he a party man. Like his
father, he thought of himself as the mediator between the King and
the factions. He preferred to get into office and govern, rather than rot
in futile opposition, and his attitude to party was a peculiar compound
of indifference and conventional eighteenth-century prejudice: in some
ways his aloofness was even old-fashioned. But his precious independence was a greater asset than ever: since he had never been a Foxite,
he could take office at the invitation of the King without betraying
any principle, or wounding any friend. He had wisely ignored all

suggestions that he should join the whigs—even in November, Fox had hoped for his adherence to the coalition. But now he could take advantage of Temple's intrigue without accepting responsibility for it: if he succeeded, he would be able to rule as he wished, within the usual conventions of constitutional practice, conventions, which, unlike his rival, he did not question.

What, in any case, were the alternatives? The defeat of the King, and his subjection to Fox? Or a return to the 'seventies, with some puppet (assuming one could be found) riveted to office by the inflexible will of the King? Pitt did not doubt that a ministry led by himself was the solution to the dilemma, whatever the manœuvres which had made it possible. Intelligent government, and enlightened reforms, were too valuable to be jeopardised by considerations of party. Pitt was the only man who could save the King from the whigs, and this gave him considerable freedom of action; but he had no intention of becoming a second North, for he knew how badly the King needed his support. Despite the uncertainties of the situation, his hopes were high.

On 19 December an expectant House of Commons heard that Pitt had taken office as First Lord of the Treasury and Chancellor of the Exchequer. Fox and North could not restrain their mirth. Pitt would go the same way as Shelburne: defeat after defeat would drive the young minister to resign. But what if an appeal should be made to the electorate? Fox denounced rumours of a dissolution, reminding the House that no one 'would say that such a prerogative ought to be exercised merely to suit the convenience of an ambitious young man'. If such an occurrence took place, he would move a formal inquiry when the new Parliament met. But the truth of the matter was that the whigs were not prepared to accept an appeal from the House to the constituencies. Burke and Fox made much of the Commons as a check upon the tyranny of the Crown, but they were less happy with a similar restraint upon the tyranny of the House. Despite all his talk of liberty, and the advanced nature of his opinions on Cabinet responsibility, Fox fumed over the dangers of 'annihilating our importance, and avowedly erecting a monarchy on the basis of an effected popularity, independent of and uncontrollable by Parliament'. He feared the alliance of the King and the East India Company: two mighty election agents united by a burning desire to crush the insolent coalition.

Nevertheless, many hesitated to join a minister whose tenure of office seemed destined to be brief, and the prospect was not improved by the resignation of Earl Temple, three days after receiving the seals as Secretary of State. For once, Pitt's aptitude for deep and refreshing sleep deserted him, and his self-confidence momentarily faltered. But, conquering his depression, he determined to go on as best he could. Temple had not resigned on any issue of high policy: he was indignant at not being granted a dukedom for his services. George III, who had decided to reserve all future dukedoms for members of the royal family, was contemptuous of his accomplice's 'base conduct', but Fox was delighted by the rift in the government. He would soon be back in office: the ministry was already breaking up. During the Christmas festivities, Pitt's Cabinet was light-heartedly dismissed as a 'mince-pie administration', and many shared Gibbon's opinion that, unless he took care, Pitt's 'pretty painted pleasure boat' would be run down by Fox's 'sooty black collier'.

Whatever the problems confronting him, Pitt made no attempt to bring Shelburne into the Cabinet. He had never identified himself unreservedly with the Shelburne interest, and the Earl's notorious unpopularity would be a severe handicap to a ministry fighting for its life. Pitt knew of the 'absolute influence of prejudice' against the former minister, and he had no wish to appear the instrument by which Shelburne could return to power. He wanted to be the actual, as well as the nominal, head of the ministry, and his loyalty during the negotiations with Fox had amply repaid any debt of gratitude which he owed. Shelburne was a difficult man to work with, and the explanation of his exclusion lies in his own character and career. In compensation for this disappointment, he was created Marquis of Lansdowne.

Whilst Robinson pressed on with his preparations for the general election, Pitt had to show hesitant Members and uncommitted patrons that he possessed the determination worthy of a minister of the Crown. It was also necessary for the passions roused by the coalition and the India Bill to be subordinated to some purpose. Some years later Pitt told Malmesbury that popular feeling could rise 'in a way not only unknown, but in a manner as if it had no concerted beginning'; but, during the winter of 1783–1784, his supporters made the most of popular prejudice against Fox. Public meetings were arranged and addresses organised, and although the minister and his colleagues felt that they were being swept along by the tide of public opinion, the indignation against the coalition—genuine as it was—was not entirely spontaneous. Pitt was careful, however, not to set himself up against the House of Commons; he was content to maintain the King's right to choose his ministers, and the necessity for the House not to condemn any minister prematurely.

When Parliament reassembled in January 1784, Pitt proclaimed his independence of 'backstairs influence': he would never condescend to be 'the instrument of any secret advisers whatever', nor would he be responsible for measures which were not his own. But he was still in a minority of thirty-nine votes. He also announced his intention of bringing forward an India Bill. This was a clever move, for he showed his awareness of the need for reform, and that this could be undertaken without violating established rights. When the Clerkship of the Pells —a sinecure worth £3,000 a year—fell vacant, Pitt, who had an obvious claim to it, proved that he was not interested in making profit for himself at the expense of the public. He refused the office, passing it instead to Barré, who accepted it in place of the pension which he had been granted by Rockingham. If Pitt's self-denial was denounced by his opponents as nothing more than a priggish piece of political legerdemain, the gesture had been made.

On 14 January, Pitt introduced his India Bill. He had taken pains to consult the Company, and the Bill embodied proposals which had been discussed at a conference with their representatives on 5 January. Despatches to India were to be scrutinised by the government, and the General Court of the Company could not reverse a decision of the Directors without the King's consent. In India, government was to be carried on by a Governor and three Councillors in each of the Presidencies. The Governor and the Commander-in-Chief were to be appointed by the Crown, the other officials by the Company, selections being ratified by the King. The Board of Control in London was to consist of the Home Secretary, the Chancellor of the Exchequer, and several other Privy Councillors. It was not to distribute the Company's patronage, but all appointments were to be supervised by it, and in order to restrain the avarice of employees in India, a tribunal was to be set up to try alleged offences.

Pitt had attempted to retain the increased measure of control which Fox had envisaged, whilst putting the vexed problem of patronage to one side. By co-operating with the Company, he had gone out of his way to refute charges that he was subverting its charter. But it was more difficult to persuade the Commons of his wisdom, and his Bill was defeated by 222 votes to 214 on 23 January. Nevertheless, he could claim that he was gradually gaining the confidence of the House, and all the while Robinson was completing his arrangements for the election. By promising whatever was most appropriate in each instance —a sinecure for an impoverished brother, or a commission for a lusty younger son—he persuaded patrons to see that their Members changed sides, or to undertake to install new representatives at the first opportunity. Many Members succumbed to this form of persuasion, as well as to Pitt's eloquence and brave stand against the coalition.

At the same time, efforts were made to bring Fox and Pitt together. The independents asked the Duke of Portland to use his influence for this purpose, and a meeting at the St. Alban's Tavern sought to substitute a new coalition for that of Fox and North. But negotiations foundered when Portland could not be satisfied that the new Cabinet would be formed on an 'equal' and 'fair' footing. Pitt did not agree that his own resignation was the necessary preliminary to any understanding with Fox, and he flatly refused to serve in any ministry which included North. Fox would not join the existing ministry: to do so would be to condone the intrigue which had given it birth. Deadlock ensued, and in the eyes of the public Fox was the more recalcitrant of the parties involved. The minister's support in the House was growing, and in desperation the whigs threatened to stop the supplies, even to reject the annual Mutiny Bill. When Pitt was granted the freedom of the City of London, his coach was attacked by a gang of hooligans as it was passing Brooks's Club after the banquet in the Grocers' Hall. The outrage discredited the whigs, and Fox was compelled publicly to deny all complicity in the affair, stating that he had been in bed with Mrs. Armistead at the time—'and the good lady is prepared to go on oath to prove it'.

By 8 March the opposition's majority in the Commons had shrunk to one vote, and on the 24th Parliament was dissolved. The election was a triumph for Pitt and Robinson: the King had correctly judged the temper of the nation. As many as 160 coalitionists lost their seats, the ministry doing particularly well in the 'open' constituencies, and Fox's martyrs became a political gibe, as well as a religious legend. When the King congratulated Pitt on his election for the University of Cambridge, he could not refrain from commenting that the returns were 'more favourable than the most sanguine could have expected'. The 'popular' character of Pitt's victory has been exaggerated, but his success was overwhelming, and he was a hero in the popular estimation. Resentment at Fox's conduct was widespread, and whilst Pitt headed the poll at Cambridge (thus fulfilling one of his early ambitions) Fox was returned at Westminster only after a tremendous struggle. In the two-Member constituency he came 460 votes behind Hood, but 236 above Wray—after Georgiana, Duchess of Devonshire, and other whig beauties, had canvassed on his behalf. As the King passed Carlton House, on his way to open the new Parliament, the Prince of Wales held a magnificent reception to celebrate his friend's election. But the story of the Westminster contest was not complete. Wray challenged the result and demanded a scrutiny, and Pitt's inexperience and logical temperament betrayed him into approving what looked like malicious persecution. His uncharitable and unimaginative tenacity only revived sympathy for the unhappy Fox, who took his seat as Member for Orkney and Shetland during the investigation. Pitt had finally to drop the inquiry, but he had appeared spiteful and vindictive, and men drew the contrast between his behaviour and Fox's generous magnanimity.

Pitt had now the confidence of the Commons as well as of the King, and it might have been anticipated that the means by which he had entered office and defeated his rival would prove too strong for that independence which he had treasured so intensely, and flaunted so flamboyantly, during his brief political career. But, however loyal he was to the King, and however obedient to accepted constitutional practice, Pitt retained his own freedom, whilst George III was glad to rely on the minister who had saved him from Fox. Pitt now turned his attention to the pressing problems of public finance and international relations, and for the next five years he was engaged in strengthening Britain's economy and prestige, as well as introducing schemes of thoughtful and practical reform. There were weightier reasons than the minister's youth for surrounding nations to stand and stare, for the kingdom flourished under his guidance. Despite disappointments and reverses, his gifts were allowed their freest expression, and his hopes their greatest measure of fulfilment, during the peacetime ministry. He was now entering the most rewarding period of his life, and the least frustrating of his career, however valiantly he later grappled with the stern trials of war and revolution. The words which he had used when defending the peace with America, in February 1783, epitomised the spirit in which he applied himself—flushed with the exultation of victory at the hustings—to the task of restoring the self-respect of a defeated nation:

> Let us examine what is left, with a manly and determined courage. Let us strengthen ourselves against inveterate enemies, and reconciliate our ancient friends. The misfortunes of individuals, and of kingdoms, that are laid open and examined with true wisdom, are more than half-redressed; and to this great object should be directed all the virtue and abilities of this House. Let us feel our calamities—let us bear them, too, like men.

3 THE PEACETIME MINISTRY
1784–1789

MANY men, more experienced than Pitt in government and administration, would have quailed before the problems which now challenged
his resource and skill. The humiliation of defeat had bequeathed a
heavy legacy of deficit and debt, which was all the more grievous
because North had raised loans on wasteful terms. With the last four
years of the conflict alone costing £80,000,000, the national debt had
soared to the astounding figure of £231,000,000, and confidence in the
government's financial stability was so feeble that Consols had sunk as
low as 57. High duties, imposed in a desperate attempt to increase
revenue, were evaded by smuggling, and there was much confusion in
a fiscal system riddled with anomalies and abuses. Besides these
monetary troubles, discontent in Ireland threatened to erupt in violence,
and in India administrative chaos was aggravated by the imminence of
reform. Gloomy spirits heard in the American catastrophe the knell of
Britain's greatness: only twenty years before, the nation had exulted
proudly in its triumph over the Bourbons. Now, without an ally on
the Continent, almost without a friend in the world, it resigned itself,
wearily and resentfully, to the loss of those colonies which, however
much they had been neglected in the past, were perversely deemed the
source of all former glory. While a handful of enthusiasts demanded
Parliamentary reform, the process which was to secure Britain's
commercial predominance continued, scarcely heeded within the
narrow world of politics. New techniques were relentlessly applied in

agriculture and industry. The construction of canals and roads facilitated communication. Enclosures changed the face of England, and revolutionised the structure of rural society by widening the gap between the prosperous tenant farmer and the landless labourer. The population multiplied, and in the north a new England took shape, as sleepy hamlets were transformed into thriving towns, whose ugliness rivalled their prosperity. But a price had to be paid. All the worst features of town life were reproduced on a larger scale, as the modern centres of industry spawned their progeny of narrow, foul-smelling streets; of insanitary hovels, populated by gaunt, overworked factory hands; of brutality, drunkenness, and vice. Life had always been hard for the poor of the towns: there were more of them now. All this was remote from the bland elegance usually associated with urban society in the eighteenth century; and the foundations of future wealth were laid in blind suffering.

Perhaps Pitt was more fortunate than he knew: in the 1780s the industrial revolution was getting under way, and the national economy, despite the colossal expense of the American War, was expanding. Yet, if the novelty of much of Pitt's fiscal policy has been exaggerated, he brought order to the nation's finances in a series of brilliant budgets. The general tendency of his policy was in favour of freer trade, and here he owed a debt to Shelburne, who had planned to introduce economic reforms in 1782, and to Adam Smith, the theorist. Pitt had read *The Wealth of Nations*, but, while he paid a gracious compliment to its author at a dinner-party in 1787—'Nay, we will stand until you are seated, for we are all your scholars'—as well as referring to his 'extensive knowledge of detail and depth of philosophical research' in his budget speech in 1792, it is probable that, at least in the early years of his ministry, he was following Shelburne's example, rather than the principles expounded by the Scots professor.

In an age when tea, rum, wine, and spirits were taxed at monstrously high rates, it was inevitable that men should seek to outwit the law, and that the lawbreaker should be benevolently regarded as a useful, if not an indispensable, member of the community. Consequently the prevalence, and popularity, of smuggling constituted a permanent drain on the revenue, and the ludicrous nature of the situation is well illustrated by the fact that, out of 13,000,000 lb. of tea consumed in England every year, no more than 5,500,000 lb. were sold by the East India Company

which held the official monopoly. The rest was conveyed by a complicated system of smuggling, and when it is remembered that tea bore
a duty of 119 per cent, the huge losses sustained by the government in
uncollected imposts become more comprehensible. Here was a situation clearly calling for immediate reform, and Pitt was of the opinion
that the surest solution lay in making smuggling less lucrative and less
attractive by reducing the duties to practicable rates, which men would
be willing to pay, and which would undercut the smuggler's price.
Duties which had theoretically brought in £700,000 a year were
therefore amended to bring in an estimated £169,000: the lower sum
was a more realistic evaluation. In addition, instead of the muddled
procedure by which one article was often liable for a multitude of
duties, he imposed a single duty on each article, and by setting up his
'Consolidated Fund' in 1787 he finally centralised and standardised
the collection and distribution of revenue. By his 'Hovering Act' he
empowered customs officials to search vessels up to four leagues out
to sea, and whenever the incumbent of any Customs House sinecure
died, he seized the opportunity of abolishing the post.

Until the new system was fully established, Pitt recognised that there
would be a temporary loss in income, and he compensated for this by
introducing new taxes, and by making fuller use of older ones—the
famous window tax, for example. Duties were imposed over the years
on hats, ribbons, horses, linens, candles, calicoes, paper, bricks, tiles,
and even servants, the distinction which was made between male and
female servants for this purpose provoking many ribald comments on
the part of Pitt's critics. An inquiry was also instituted into 'fees,
gratuities, perquisites, and emoluments', and instead of the inefficient
and corrupt methods which had usually been adopted whenever the
government sought a loan, Pitt established the system of raising loans
by tender, and the impartial auditing of public accounts. The privilege
of franking mail, abused as well as enjoyed by Members of Parliament,
was more strictly limited, but it was impossible to prevent the misuse
of this immunity, which was eventually abolished in 1840. So successful were these measures that an annual deficit was converted into a
surplus, and the minister, encouraged by their outcome, proceeded to
tackle the recurring problem of the national debt.

In a less sophisticated age, no one was reconciled to the perpetual
existence of the national debt. It was thought an affront to the national

honour, as well as a grim gift to posterity, to allow the amount to accumulate, and throughout the eighteenth century schemes had been devised to pay off the debt over a number of years. A multitude of arm-chair chancellors, sublimely inexperienced in administrative matters, propounded theories of redemption, usually invoking the magical properties of compound interest. In 1773 the Reverend Dr. Richard Price, the prominent Unitarian, published his *Appeal on the National Debt*, arguing the case for an inalienable Sinking Fund, and though he was not the first to make the suggestion, he was possibly the most plausible. Many economists and financiers, amateur and professional, examined the project, frequently adding their own refinements. Pitt, who had a greater interest in economic theory than in political speculation, took over the basic idea, and when he brought forward his version in 1786, Price claimed that 'the plan which Mr. Pitt has adopted is that which I have been writing about and recommending for years'. But his bitterness at Pitt's failure to make any public acknowledgment had obscured Price's insight: the two schemes were not identical. If the principle was the same—the annual investment of a sum of money in order to clear the national debt by the accumulation of compound interest—there was a significant difference in the way the money was to be obtained. Price advocated borrowing money at simple interest, in order to invest at compound interest. Pitt proposed to set aside £1,000,000 every year from the national revenue: he did not wish to raise an additional loan. During its early years the scheme helped to restore public faith in the financial integrity of the government, as well as paying off several millions, and it is important to differentiate between its operation before the war with revolutionary France, and the necessity during hostilities to borrow money for the same purpose. The Sinking Fund was universally approved: even Fox gave it his blessing, and, as late as 1806, Lord Henry Petty, who had succeeded Pitt at the Exchequer, defended it as the means by which the nation had been saved from greater financial burdens, describing it as 'an advantage gained by nothing'. Pitt was not alone in falling for the charms of compound interest—the financier's equivalent of the philosopher's stone.

In 1784, when Alderman Saw' ridge brought forward his annual motion calling for Parliamentary reform, Pitt asked him not to press the matter, as he himself intended to make proposals of his own, in due

12   BURTON PYNSENT
From an engraving by T. Bonnor, 1786

13   BOWLING-GREEN HOUSE, PUTNEY, WHERE WILLIAM PITT DIED ON 23 JANUARY 1806
From a nineteenth-century engraving

14 WILLIAM PITT'S WATCH
Now in the Fitzwilliam Museum, Cambridge

15 WILLIAM PITT'S PORT-GLASS
*Now in the Pitt Room, Barclay's
Bank, Bene't Street, Cambridge*

course. Sawbridge ignored his request, but Pitt nevertheless voted for his motion, which was defeated. In April 1785 he laid his own scheme for the reform of Parliamentary representation before the Commons. He had promised the Reverend Christopher Wyvill, the leader of the Yorkshire reformers, that he would 'exert his whole power and credit, as a man and as a minister', but Wyvill was mistaken in assuming that the Bill would be a governmental measure. Parliamentary reform was so controversial, and Pitt's position in the House so unpredictable (even after a victory as overwhelming as that of 1784), that it was impossible to throw the entire weight of the ministry behind the movement for reform. The King distrusted any meddling with the constitution, and within the Cabinet opinion was divided, Thurlow, the Lord Chancellor, being especially vehement in denouncing any alteration in the system of representation. The opposition was equally confused: there was no more zealous advocate of reform than Fox, no more vigorous opponent than Burke. The Members of the Commons were particularly sensitive in a matter which so closely affected their own interests, and all that Pitt could do was to hope that his support, urged from the front bench, and embodied in specific proposals, would convince a sufficient number of the necessity and the wisdom of reform. At the same time, though he was doubtful of the chances of immediate success, Pitt was confident that reform would ultimately prevail in both the British and Irish legislatures. Writing to his friend, the Duke of Rutland, now Lord-Lieutenant in Dublin, he confessed that 'Parliamentary reform, I am still sure, . . . must sooner or later be carried in both countries. If it is well done, the sooner the better.'

Pitt's proposals have been censured for yielding too much to the proprietors, and to the spirit which thought of seats in Parliament as private property, rather than a trust on behalf of the people. But Pitt had already experienced the complacent stolidity of most Members towards any attempt to modify the existing state of affairs, and, in their moderation and restraint, his proposals met the usual criticism that reform was impracticable. He was seeking, not merely to sound the prospects for reform, but to achieve a degree of emendation which would be immediately effective. He wanted to disfranchise thirty-six of the most corrupt boroughs, and to give the seventy-six seats thus vacated to the cities of London and Westminster, and to the large and under-represented counties. Nor was this all: £1,000,000 were to be paid to the proprietors in compensation, each borough being asked to apply for disfranchisement by a petition from two-thirds of its electorate. This procedure would make continuous reform possible, as further boroughs sank into decay. In the counties, the copyholders were to be admitted to the franchise, Pitt claiming that 'such an accession to the body of electors would give fresh energy to Representation'. Dundas and Wilberforce spoke in favour of the Bill, the latter returning from Nice for the occasion, and though Fox disapproved of the payment to the borough-mongers, he gave the measure general support. But all was in vain: Pitt was defeated by 248 votes to 174, a substantial reverse when he had done so much to conciliate the die-hards on both sides of the House. He felt his disappointment keenly, and he was never to introduce further proposals for the reform of the legislature. It is too simple to suggest that he used reform merely to facilitate his rise to power, only to throw it over once it had served its turn. In eighteenth-century politics reforming notions were more of a liability than an asset, and it would be difficult to show precisely how Pitt's career had been advanced in this way. It is nearer the truth to say that, with his practical outlook, he was tired of spending time and labour in preparing schemes which the Commons seemed determined to reject, without even the consolation of a fair hearing. He had attempted reform both as a private Member and as a minister; and, faced with the hostility of the King, of many members of his Cabinet, and of the majority of the Lords and Commons, he realised the futility of pressing for measures which had no hope of success. Busy as he was, with the day-to-day tasks of government, he postponed new exertions in the cause of Parliamentary reform until more auspicious times. But, when a fresh Parliament was elected in 1790, the French Revolution had already cast its baleful influence on all hopes of reform in England. It is attractive—but somewhat Pharisaical—blithely to applaud Grey's youthful idealism in calling for the reform of Parliament, at the height of the struggle with revolutionary France, whilst spurning Pitt as a turncoat and a hypocrite. But he had never been an 'abstract' reformer: he was interested in results, not colourful fictions. He believed that circumstances altered cases, and it is dangerous to read back into earlier stages of his career the attitudes of the anti-Jacobin period.

But there were more urgent problems than the reform of Parliament. The situation in Ireland was ominous. Despite the temporary relief which had followed the granting of legislative independence, that unhappy island was still divided by bitter enmities and violent antagonisms. Grattan and Flood, vying with each other in vindictive eloquence, pursued their brilliant rivalry in the Parliament on College Green; and, within the Volunteers, Charlemont and Bristol (the Bishop of Derry) clashed over the emancipation of the Catholics, the prelate supporting their claims for enfranchisement. While Flood pressed for the reform of the Irish Parliament, the country languished in the grip of distress. Despite the efforts of both the Catholic and Protestant clergy, the 'Whiteboys' became ever more popular, the savage protest of an oppressed and unenlightened people. Public order hovered on the brink of chaos, and in August 1785 Rutland described Dublin as 'in great measure under the domination of the mob'.

Pitt strove to ameliorate hardship. As early as October 1784 he had told Rutland:

> I own to you that the line to which my mind at present inclines is to give Ireland an almost unlimited communication of commercial advantages, if we can receive in return some security that her strength and riches will be our benefit, and that she will contribute from time to time in their increasing proportions to the common exigencies of the empire.

In May the Irish House of Commons had addressed the King for 'a wise and well-digested plan for a liberal arrangement of a commercial intercourse between Great Britain and Ireland', and Pitt, doubtless influenced by Adam Smith's plea for a union with Ireland, coupled with free trade between the two kingdoms, hoped that even in the absence of political union, economic reform would circumvent the vexed (and apparently insoluble) problem of religion: the Irish, Catholic and Protestant alike, clung to their convictions with the ardour of a less benevolent, and less indifferent, age.

Characteristically, Pitt took advice from those he thought best qualified to give it: Foster, the Irish Chancellor of the Exchequer; Beresford, the Chief Commissioner for Revenue; and Orde, the Secretary for Ireland, who urged him to 'act . . . with the utmost liberality consistent with your own safety: it must in the long run be the wisest policy'. In February 1785 proposals were submitted to the Irish Parliament. Pitt suggested that foreign and colonial products should pass between Britain and Ireland without an increase in duty;

that the products of both countries should be imported free, or at the lower of the two duties in force; that all prohibitions on trade between Ireland and the United Kingdom should lapse; and that when the Irish revenue exceeded £656,000 a year the surplus should go to the upkeep of the navy. These propositions were not received uncritically in Dublin, Grattan insisting that no contribution should be made to the maintenance of the navy until the Irish deficit had been cleared, but they passed both Houses, and were then ready for consideration at Westminster.

They were at once subjected to much hostile criticism, which was as ill-informed as it was irresponsible. Many were incensed that the proposals had been laid, in the first instance, before the Irish Parliament, and Fox and his colleagues opposed them on the grounds that they would mean the ruin of British industry. In Manchester, Glasgow, Paisley, and Bristol, as well as other towns, addresses were voted against the Irish resolutions, and Fox, relishing an unwonted and scarcely deserved popularity as the defender of the manufacturing interest, was fêted in Manchester—a town which had been foremost in denouncing him a year before. In the face of this tumult, Pitt modified his proposals. He added a clause stipulating that, in future, the Irish Parliament would have to enact all laws passed at Westminster which regulated trade between the two countries. (This was interpreted by the Irish as a sinister attack on the recent concession of legislative independence.) The monopoly of the East India Company was to be maintained; the Navigation Laws, now hailed by the whigs as the foundations of British prosperity, were to be binding in both kingdoms; duties were not to be reduced below 10½ per cent; and the Irish request that their budget should be balanced before any part of their revenue was diverted towards the needs of the Admiralty was rejected.

But, though the government had endured the tantrums of British manufacturers whose concern for their country's welfare was identified with an anxiety for their own profits, they had now to face onslaughts on their integrity, once the Irish were confronted with the emasculated resolutions. The English whigs, inspired by party zeal and virulent memories, sought the defeat of the government in the Irish Parliament, and those who had so recently feared for the future of England declared their solicitude for the welfare of Ireland. 'I will not barter

English commerce for Irish slavery!' Fox cried, in a piece of humbug which ensured neither English prosperity nor Irish freedom. Whatever his other virtues, financial acumen was not one of them, and he scoffed gaily at economic theories; but he succeeded in his main object. The reception given to the revised resolutions was so boisterous that they were never formally introduced in Dublin, and Pitt's first attempt to deal with the Irish problem was foiled by misrepresentation, ignorant self-interest, and factious animosity. The proposals for free trade with Ireland became part of that 'history of eminently wise and enlightened ideas, abandoned at the first sign of difficulty or unpopularity'. But, however bewitching, Lecky's sneer is unjust: the strength of the opposition to Pitt's proposals must not be underestimated. If modification failed to meet his opponents' fury, what other means could he adopt? To talk of resignation implies that the political conventions of the day were those of the twentieth century, and, in any case, if Pitt had resigned, a crisis of the gravest dimensions would have been precipitated. If Ireland was allowed to 'drift to disaster', the responsibility lies chiefly with those who opposed Pitt's reforms, who unscrupulously exploited every prejudice, both at Dublin and Westminster, in order to gratify their desire to inflict a reverse upon the government, irrespective of the merits of the legislation involved.

The eighteenth article of the Treaty of Versailles had called for the appointment of commissioners to prepare a commercial agreement between England and France, 'on the basis of reciprocity and mutual convenience', and had laid down a time-limit of two years, during which the requirement was to be implemented. Shelburne had contemplated such a scheme, and on the French side it was vigorously pressed by Vergennes, whose profuse affirmations of friendship were allied to diplomatic subtlety, but, in the confusion following Shelburne's fall, the proposed treaty was forgotten. But, as the months lengthened into years, the French became impatient. Increasingly suspicious of British good faith, they were willing to use powerful means of reminding His Majesty's Government of its obligations under the peace treaty. Vergennes raised the duties on British manufactures, and then prohibited the import of iron, steel, cutlery, cottons, and linens. This severity stung British memories, as well as striking at British pockets, and after the failure of the Irish proposals, Pitt turned his attention to the French. He was fortunate in having at his disposal a knowledgeable and astute negotiator in William Eden, who, with calm indifference to party loyalty, had changed sides a second time to better his own prospects. In March 1786 Eden left for Paris, but before his departure he heard up-to-date evidence on the condition of British manufactures and the balance of trade, and he was consequently better equipped than his French counterparts to drive a hard and advantageous bargain.

On 26 September 1786 the treaty was signed. Citizens of both countries were given freedom to do business in the other, without incurring any liability for taxation, or any restraint on the practice of their religion. Duties on French wines, vinegar, and oil were reduced. French silks were prohibited, and linens admitted at low rates. English hardware and cutlery carried a duty of 10 per cent; cottons, woollens, muslins, saddlery, porcelain, and pottery one of 12 per cent. Beer bore a high duty of 30 per cent. Both governments undertook to suppress smuggling, and to revise the treaty after twelve years.

Unlike the Irish proposals, the treaty was popular in Britain, partly because it represented the wishes of the manufacturers, who had been consulted before and during the negotiations. But, whilst Dorset complimented Eden on his good work, Fox and his friends attacked the agreement in violent language. Fox could easily drop the disinterested and far-sighted tone which is so often invoked as proof of his statesmanship, and his speeches on the Eden treaty show him at his worst. His description of France as Britain's natural foe drew upon him a rebuke in Pitt's haughtiest vein:

> To suppose that any nation could be unalterably the enemy of another is weak and childish. It had neither its foundation in the experience of nations nor in the history of men. It . . . supposed the existence of diabolical malice in the original frame of man. . . .

Pitt could afford to ignore the cheap gibes that he was betraying his father's memory in seeking friendly relations with France. He had the manufacturing interest with him, this time, and Eden, whatever sarcasms he bore from his ex-associates, had performed his duties with immense skill. The treaty was greatly to Britain's advantage, for she was much better equipped than her neighbour to enjoy the risky privilege of free trade. Her industries, already benefiting from the primary stages of the industrial revolution, swamped the French

market, and the treaty was justified, in British eyes, by that most
elusive, but unanswerable, argument—success. For the French the
results were less happy. Unemployment rose in the industrial areas, and
in towns like Abbeville, Amiens, Lille, and Lyons the treaty was hated
as the cause of unmitigated affliction. Already embarrassed financially,
the French had the misfortune to suffer a bad harvest in 1788, and their
woes were complicated by the unwholesome policies of Calonne and
Brienne, by the obstinacy of the nobles in resisting reform, and by the
short-sightedness of the Parlements in obstructing every initiative on
the part of the Crown. Several years later, Robespierre claimed that,
by the commercial treaty, England had deliberately precipitated the
French Revolution; an exaggerated and misleading assertion, but one
which vividly illustrates the impression which Eden's triumph made
on the minds of intelligent Frenchmen. The treaty was a convenient
bogy, the obvious explanation of ills whose causes lay deeper, and
many Frenchmen, conscious only of a crisis which threatened to
culminate in disaster, allowed prejudice to cloud their minds. Originally, Pitt had been suspicious of the zeal with which the French had
sought a commercial agreement: now the tables were turned, and the
French saw themselves as the victims of unnatural guile. The treaty was
repudiated by the Convention before it had run more than half of its
course: in normal conditions it would have been interesting to see
whether the French would have pressed as keenly for its renewal as
they had clamoured for its inception.

During the eighteenth century the Slave Trade was generally regarded
as indispensable to national prosperity. The *asiento* clause of the Treaty
of Utrecht had been prized because it helped Britain's participation in
the traffic, and as profits swelled consciences slept. Liverpool thrived
on the transportation of slaves, and any feelings of uneasiness were
soothed by agreeable philanthropists, who justified the trade on
humanitarian grounds, as a beneficent activity, which saved many
savages from the horrors of barbarism. But, as the scandals of the voyage
became known, a small, articulate body of opinion began to agitate,
first for the regulation and then for the abolition of the trade. The
Quakers denounced the commerce in slaves, and disowned all who
participated in it, and the abolitionists took heart in 1772, when
Mansfield ruled that any slave who landed on British soil became a free
man. The Evangelical and Methodist revivals led men to question a

form of business which contrasted so harshly with the precepts of Christianity, and in 1787 Granville Sharp founded the Abolitionist Society. Wilberforce had inquired into the conditions of the trade, and one day, as he and Pitt talked beneath an oak-tree in the garden at Holwood, he told his friend of his intention of raising the issue in the Commons. When the time came Wilberforce was ill, and Pitt himself introduced the motion calling for an inquiry into the Slave Trade, on 9 May 1788. He had already tried, during the negotiations for the Eden treaty, to win the co-operation of the French government in suppressing 'the villainous traffic now carried on in Africa', but Montmorin's reactions had been tepid and discouraging. Pitt did not take any of the credit which was due to Wilberforce, and Fox responded with characteristic generosity. But even before general discussion of the subject began, Sir William Dolben introduced a Bill regulating the conditions under which slaves were transported. He had been horrified by the plight in which he had seen slaves on board ships lying in the Thames, and he felt obliged to take action.

The slave traders replied with vigour. The Liverpool merchants taunted the abolitionists with contriving not only their ruin but the destruction of the national economy. The commercial advantages of the trade were cited against the allegedly illusory benefits of abolition. If British ships ceased to carry slaves, those of other nations would continue to do so; there would be no improvement in the Negroes' condition, there might even be a deterioration. Dolben's Bill was unrealistic, for the slaves enjoyed a higher standard of living on the voyage to the West Indies and America than that which they had known in Africa. Nevertheless, the measure passed the Commons, only to receive a severe mauling in the Lords, where Thurlow excelled himself: he was bitterly opposed to the pernicious antics of starry-eyed idealists. The Bill became law only after it had been mangled by the zealous guardians of commercial supremacy.

When Wilberforce reintroduced his motion in May 1789 he encountered stern resistance, and the delaying tactics of the conservative interest were difficult to surmount. No decision was reached, and the question was postponed for a year. And so it went on throughout the 1790s. Wilberforce was constantly thwarted, and events in San Domingo strengthened his opponents, who claimed that the retention of the trade was absolutely necessary, when reform issued in violence

and bloodshed. As the revolution in France monopolised public attention, the prospects of reform faded, and Pitt, preoccupied with more
momentous affairs, advocated caution because of the state of public
opinion. His relations with Wilberforce cooled in consequence. Yet,
when the subject came before the Commons in April 1792 he made one
of his greatest speeches, eloquently pleading the case for total abolition.
The House admired his oratory, but rejected his logic, and many
Members, seeking a solution which would salve their consciences
without endangering their prosperity, settled for Dundas's compromise
—the regulation of the trade, as a first step towards final abolition,
which remained conveniently remote. There the matter rested: it was
left to Fox and Grenville to carry abolition in 1806.

Pitt's conduct has been criticised as weak and excessively cautious,
but would the outcome have been any different if he had made abolition a part of ministerial policy? Could he have staked the fate of his
administration on such an issue? First, he needed to persuade many of
his Cabinet colleagues of the wisdom of the step: Sydney and Thurlow
were both opposed to abolition, and when Dolben's Bill was debated
in the Lords, Richmond was the only minister to speak in its defence.
Abolition, like Parliamentary reform, defied the usual party divisions,
imprecise, unpredictable, and unstable as these were. Lax organisation
and slack (often barely perceptible) discipline made it impossible for
Pitt to impose his own point of view on reluctant followers. All he
could do—all he thought it right to do—was to give a lead which he
hoped would be followed. His own attitude towards political combina-
tions was conservative: he had no wish to create a party in anything
like the modern sense. Nor could he overlook the King's suspicions,
for George III, under Thurlow's surly influence, regarded abolition
with a jaundiced eye. Had Thurlow succeeded in defeating Dolben's
Bill in the Lords, Pitt had made up his mind that he and the Lord
Chancellor could not remain in the same Cabinet; but this was a
determination to force Thurlow's resignation, not a threat to tender
his own. With his high sense of duty, and his own conviction that he
was fitted for power, resignation did not come easily to Pitt's mind,
and it is difficult to see what it would have accomplished.

But, if a less cautious attitude might have influenced some members
of the Cabinet, it would not have persuaded many Members of the
Commons to vote against their own interests. Even as doughty a

reformer as Alderman Sawbridge gave way to the entreaties of his constituents and opposed abolition. And it was impossible for Pitt to force through abolition during the 'nineties, when the Jacobin scare was at its peak, when interest in the Slave Trade was declining because fewer slaves were being carried in British ships, and when he himself, burdened with the immense responsibilities of the war, had little time to spare for the cause. Gloomily he became convinced that neither the state of opinion in Parliament nor prevalent feeling in the country at large favoured abolition. To censure him for failing to resign is to ignore the realities of the situation: there was little similarity between his position over the Slave Trade and that which he took up over the Irish Union and Catholic Emancipation. He shrank from precipitating a major political crisis on such an issue, and during the first decade of the war Fox was considered as little better than a traitor by the majority of his countrymen, and was wholly unacceptable to the King as an alternative minister. The simple truth is, that Pitt could not procure the passage of legislation which, whatever its merits in the opinion of posterity, was repugnant to the King, to many members of the Cabinet, and to the majority of Lords and Commons. There was no technique by which such a feat could be accomplished: there was no short cut to success.

Soon after his triumph in the 1784 election, Pitt turned his attention to Indian affairs. He brought forward and passed a Bill embodying the proposals which he had unsuccessfully submitted to Parliament earlier in the year. The Board of Control was set up, and the system established which, despite many imperfections, governed India until the Mutiny made further reform imperative. But the enemies of Warren Hastings had also been active, and when the Governor returned to England in 1785, in high hopes of a peerage, Burke gave notice of a motion of censure. Despite the sympathy of the King, and the general support of the ministry, Hastings could not escape the attentions of his foes, who were determined to call him to account, and the incompetence with which his case was handled only provoked more attacks and inquiries. Burke again returned to the offensive, and there was enough substance in the charges to make investigation inevitable: Hastings's conduct in India had often been high-handed as well as brusquely efficient, and provided his critics with a plentiful supply of material. Pitt appreciated Hastings's achievements and was concerned for his welfare, but he thought the fine imposed on Cheyt Singh excessive, and by voting for the Benares charge he made impeachment certain. Hastings, who had anticipated the unquestioning support of the minister, considered himself betrayed, and petulantly accused Pitt and Dundas of envy and deceit. Pitt's motives were more honourable and more complex. The facts, cited by the opposition with commendable enthusiasm, if dubious sincerity, were sufficiently suspicious, and the wave of criticism was so intense that it had to be met at some point. Hastings had offended many men during his tenure of power, and it was impossible for their accusations to be lightly dismissed. And, in addition to all these political needs, Wilberforce's more personal arguments counted for much with the minister. In 1788, with all the splendour of a long disused but magnificent ceremony, and adorned with the brilliant rhetoric of Burke, Fox, and Sheridan, the impeachment of Warren Hastings began in Westminster Hall.

The whigs hoped to inflict a severe reverse upon the ministry. Burke was passionately convinced that a verdict against Hastings was necessary for the better government of India, and for the vindication of British justice: his enthusiasm made him an unrelenting and ardent prosecutor. Fox and Sheridan were less high-minded. To them the impeachment was a valuable political manœuvre, little more, and when it failed to reach a quick conclusion they soon tired of it. The longer its duration, the more questionable was its utility. But the interminable succession of charges dragged on, and the prolixity of the evidence became meaningless. Before the end of the year Sheridan was heartily sick of the whole rigmarole, confessing to the Duchess of Devonshire that he wished Warren Hastings would run away, and Burke after him. But Burke felt himself bound by ties of honour: only the India business prevented him from giving in to his growing longing for retirement, as he became ever more isolated within the whig opposition. The tedious and involved hearing did not end until 1795, when the Lords formally acquitted an impoverished and exhausted Hastings. No one had expected it to last as long: Hastings had anticipated a speedy acquittal, Burke a prompt condemnation. The great trial had dwindled into a squalid legal persecution, forgotten by the public. Its greatest achievement was the embitterment of the former Governor-General. But, though the impeachment was marred by the pettiness of faction, it had demonstrated that the rulers of India could be called upon to justify their actions. As a warning, if nothing else, it had considerable significance.

Pitt's foreign policy was devoted towards ending the dangerous isolation which had done so much to bring the country to its knees during the American War. The commercial treaty with France, despite the initial caution he showed in his dealings with Vergennes and Montmorin, was part of a wider scheme: the reconciliation of old foes. Nor did he confine his attention to Britain's traditional enemy. He looked towards Prussia and Holland, powers with whom Britain had had previous ties and common interests. The neutrality of Frederick the Great during the 1770s, and the hostility of the Netherlands during the American War, had emphasised the coolness which had grown up between old friends, but in 1787 the Dutch crisis paved the way towards a new understanding. The feud between the Stadtholder and the Republican party reached a climax. William V was feeble and uninspiring, but he resisted any move to diminish his status or weaken his power, and his high-spirited and courageous Prussian wife was determined to fight for her husband's privileges with every available weapon. The situation was made all the more complex by the support given by the French to the Republicans, and Britain, always suspicious of any attempt to dominate the Low Countries, immediately took alarm. Sir James Harris, the ambassador at The Hague, vigorously backed up the pleas for help sent by the Princess of Orange to George III, and the energetic Princess also begged for assistance from her brother, Frederick William II of Prussia. But that indolent monarch, who was commonly said to possess not the wisdom of Solomon but his partiality for concubines, paid little heed to his sister's entreaties.

Harris reminded Pitt that, if Britain stood idly by, France would 'acquire what she had always considered as the climax of her power', and Carmarthen, the Foreign Secretary, echoed his warnings. Pitt hesitated. He had no wish to jeopardise the recent amicable relations with France, or to become embroiled in the internal affairs of another country. He told the Cabinet of his doubts on the wisdom of a bellicose policy:

> I own the immense importance of Holland being preserved as an indepen-
> dent State. It is certainly an object of the greatest magnitude. I have no
> hesitation as to what ought to be done if we do anything at all; but if we
> do anything we must make up our minds in the first instance to go to war

as a possible, though not a probable, event. Now the mere possibility is enough to make it necessary for England to reflect before she stirs. It is to be maturely weighed whether anything could repay the disturbing that state of growing affluence and prosperity in which she now is, and whether this is not increasing so fast as to make her the equal to meet any force France could collect some years hence.

Here Pitt was showing understandable reluctance to throw away the benefits which he had laboured so hard to attain: the risks involved in another war were great, and its outcome necessarily uncertain. His confidence in the country's economic resources was justified, but during the war against revolutionary France it was the source of many illusions.

The Cabinet decided to send £20,000 to help the Stadtholder: the French government was paying subsidies to the Republican party. Relations with France became strained. Vergennes, the advocate of the commercial treaty with England, had died in February 1787, and Montmorin, his successor at the French foreign ministry, was less disposed to nurse the *entente*. Frederick William shrank from taking any action, but he was jolted out of his lethargy by a personal insult inflicted on his sister. While trying to make her way to The Hague she had been detained by the Republicans and then sent back to Nijmegen. The King of Prussia demanded an apology, and mobilised an army in the Rhineland under the command of the Duke of Brunswick. The French retaliated by promising assistance to the Dutch in the event of Prussian intervention, and pressed on with their own military pre-cautions. Pitt reaffirmed British support for the Stadtholder. Forty ships-of-the-line were held in readiness for any emergency, and despatches were sent to India, containing instructions to be followed should hostilities break out. But, despite these measures, Pitt hoped that a peaceful solution would be found, perhaps by mediation on the part of the great powers:

> Could such a good understanding be agreed on, there can be little doubt that the affairs of Holland would be settled in an amicable way, to the satisfaction of all those who are interested in the welfare of the Republic.

Meanwhile, two requests for an apology to the King of Prussia had been rejected and on 13 September Prussian troops crossed the frontier. Their advance was little more than a triumphal procession; they were favourably received almost everywhere, and Republican resistance collapsed. Pitt was elated with the news:

> The business abroad is at length come to a point, and with every appearance of success. France has . . . notified . . . us that she will give assistance to the province of Holland, and we are therefore under the necessity of preparing with vigour. . . . But there seems still every reason to think France will quickly give way, as she has no army prepared, and in the meantime the Duke of Brunswick's success is in a manner decisive. News came last night that most of the towns in Holland had surrendered without any resistance. A complete revolution had taken place at The Hague, and the States of Holland had resolved to restore the Stadtholder to all his rights, and invited him back to The Hague. . . . If the issue there is as favourable as may be expected, every effort the French can make will come too late; and they will hardly engage in an unpromising contest for a mere point of honour. . . .

The French, faced with the defeat of their party in the Netherlands, divided amongst themselves on the issue of peace or war, and casting a wary glance in the direction of eastern Europe where Austria was about to join Russia in attacking Turkey, accepted the reverse, and resigned themselves to the inevitable. In October they formally renounced all hostile intent towards the new Dutch government: a humiliating confession of the utter failure of their policy in the Netherlands.

In the following year the Triple Alliance completed what the Dutch crisis had begun: Britain signed defensive treaties with both Prussia and Holland. The integrity of the United Provinces was guaranteed, and the allies promised to help each other if attacked. Pitt's wisdom in restraining the more belligerent members of the Cabinet had been justified by events, and Harris, whose genius for negotiation had done much to make the alliance possible, was raised to the peerage as Lord Malmesbury. With increasing prosperity at home, Pitt had achieved greater security abroad. But in France the diplomatic defeat sustained in Holland added to the embarrassments surrounding the administration, and the reverse was bitterly resented by those who saw English policy lurking behind every misfortune: first the Eden treaty, then the Dutch crisis.

The summer of 1788 saw Pitt at the summit of his power, but the autumn brought the threat of calamity. George III, whose health had caused some concern during June and August, collapsed at the end of October, the victim of insanity. Whilst the King raved against his family, and applied himself to imaginary business, the doctors vainly strove to cure him by the application of poultices, purgatives, and powders, as well as by regular bleedings; but he remained mad and incapable of performing his duties. No one knew how long his incapacity would last. Some prophesied the speedy accession of the Prince of Wales as George IV; others hoped for a miraculous restoration of the King's senses. The whigs were exultant: under the patronage of the Prince they would embark on a long and secure tenure of office. The ills of the coalition would be forgotten in the contented enjoyment of the sweets of success. Their leaders were scattered far and wide, but no one in the whig camp doubted that they would soon be gloating over the discomfiture of William Pitt. If there was a Regency they would still triumph, for the Prince would be appointed to exercise the royal powers during his father's illness.

But who was to be Regent? What were his powers? How was he to be appointed? Unfortunately for Fox and his friends, the constitutional position was ambiguous. If precedents were to be followed, they required interpretation, and the Prince's notorious partiality for the whigs introduced an additional complication. Since 1783 he had devoted himself enthusiastically to the whig cause, and his friendship with Charles James Fox intensified the King's disgust at his son's personal conduct and political principles. The Prince—a gifted, but selfish, young man, with a taste for pleasure and expensive amusement —had provoked trouble over his debts in 1787, the Duke of Portland falling out with him in consequence; and by his marriage in December 1785 with Mrs. Fitzherbert, a Catholic widow, in defiance of Fox's warnings, he had incurred the penalties of both the Act of Settlement and the Royal Marriages Act. The secret was poorly kept, and persistent rumours hinted that the Prince was married. Pamphleteers demanded, often in the coarsest language, whether or not the heir to the throne was married to a Papist, and since Carlton House was the social centre of the whig opposition, Fox and his colleagues became involved in the sorry tale. When Rolle raised the subject of the Fitzherbert marriage in the Commons in April 1787 Fox denied it outright; but this only meant that his influence over the Prince waned, for Mrs. Fitzherbert was an honest woman, and she never forgave him for what she considered nothing less than a base calumny on her good name. When Sheridan was called in to defend her honour by a subsequent statement the party's embarrassment was evident to everyone. Fox and the Prince were on distant terms for a year, and for a brief period while his debts were being settled the Prince, whose attitude towards political issues was determined solely by personal considerations, spoke well of Pitt, an incident which inspired many reports of negotiation during the Regency crisis.

The whigs were in a dismal plight, with both Fox and Portland estranged from the Prince, on whose influence so much depended. Burke, ever more lonely since Rockingham's death, played little part in the councils of the party, and his isolation was heightened by his profoundly personal interpretation of the constitutional aspects of the Regency: an interpretation which few of his colleagues understood. But when the news of the King's breakdown was officially confirmed in November 1788, the whigs confidently expected their problems to be solved by the Prince's immediate assumption of the royal authority, and old quarrels were hastily, if not always sincerely, made up. Yet, in reality, the crisis only aggravated their troubles, and it is not surprising that a party so deeply involved in the alienation of the King and his son should fail to appreciate the nature and significance of the technicalities of Regency. The assumption that there was an 'obvious' and 'simple' answer betrayed them into indiscretions which it proved impossible to retract, and misled them into a controversy for which they were not prepared.

Pitt resolutely faced the prospect of returning to the Bar, but he remembered his responsibilities as first minister. Should he be compelled to leave office, he determined to do so on terms which would be honourable, and which would minimise the damage the whigs could do during what he hoped would be a temporary enjoyment of power. He was also sincerely concerned to discover the correct constitutional procedure. He studied precedent carefully, and obtained reliable medical opinions on the King's condition. While he took his stand, methodically and deliberately, several members of the government prepared to desert him. Thurlow, in particular, engaged in obscure and intricate intrigues with Sheridan, whose influence over the Prince was dominant during Fox's absence on the Continent, 'rambling, no one knew where, in the arms of faded beauty'. Pitt was convinced that the

16　WILLIAM PITT AND HIS OPPONENT, CHARLES JAMES FOX, IN THE HOUSE OF COMMONS
From a contemporary drawing

17　BRITANNIA BETWEEN SCYLLA AND CHARYBDIS, OR THE VESSEL OF THE CONSTITUTION
STEERED CLEAR OF THE ROCK OF DEMOCRACY AND THE WHIRLPOOL OF ARBITRARY POWER

(Pitt steers Britannia safely to the Haven of Public Happiness, pursued by Fox,
Priestley, and Sheridan)

From a caricature by James Gillray, 1793

responsibility for supplying the exigency lay with Parliament, and that the legislature had the right to restrict the Regent's powers: there were good precedents for this point of view in the fifteenth, seventeenth, and eighteenth centuries. The best method of conferring his powers upon the Regent was more uncertain; but Pitt decided that an Act of Parliament was most appropriate, although it was not without problems, especially with regard to the royal assent. He never forgot that a Regent was a substitute for the sick King, no more, and that George III's legitimate rights had to be secured, for, on his recovery, he would resume his place as head of State. The minister was well equipped for any eventuality. If the King recovered within a few months, the opportunity for the whigs to perpetuate their own power would have been severely limited. If the King's illness lasted for a long time, the government could be carried on efficiently, for the Regent's powers were adequate for any emergency. When Dr. Willis, a clergyman who kept an asylum in Lincolnshire, assumed responsibility for the royal invalid in December, Pitt found that the most knowledgeable of the doctors was optimistic about the chances of recovery. The gloomy expectations of November gave way to sober confidence and calm hope.

On the other side, Edmund Burke fumed in impotent anguish at the hesitancies and confusions amongst the leaders of the opposition. Portland, as stolid and slow-witted as ever, gave no guidance to his followers, and though he made up his quarrel with the Prince he did so in an ungracious fashion. Loughborough, who saw the Lord Chancellorship slipping away from him as the negotiation with Thurlow proceeded, argued that the Prince had an inherent right to the Regency, which Parliament had no choice but to recognise. He also called upon the Prince to take the initiative in notifying the two Houses of the King's indisposition, and in supplying the deficiency, but this was too dangerous a step to commend itself to other members of the party. Sheridan shunned public controversy: it would be far better to get into office as quickly as possible, whatever the terms, for awkward restrictions could be disposed of once the party had established itself. Fox, whose frantic journey from Italy resulted in sickness and debilitation, veered between these various points of view. Like Sheridan he wanted to get into office: he was now almost forty years of age, and the delights of opposition had palled long ago. Only through power could he find fulfilment. But, partly because he sympathised with Loughborough's desire to be Lord Chancellor, he was also attracted to the concept of inherent right, though he shrank from the practical consequences implied in the doctrine. He failed to supply the vigorous example which was needed to stop the party from sinking into deeper confusion: there was little cohesion amongst its leaders. Both Sir Gilbert Elliot and the Duchess of Devonshire lamented the want of foresight and lack of consultation which allowed great decisions to be made by accident, not design.

The consequences of this became apparent when Pitt called for the appointment of a committee to examine precedents. Fox, irritated by what he considered a cheap ruse to delay his own entry into office, rashly denied the relevance of any precedents whatever, and asserted the Prince's right to the Regency in language which was as vague as it was extreme:

> What were they going to search for? Not for precedents upon their journals, not Parliamentary precedents, but precedents in the history of England. He would be bold to say, nay they all knew, that the doing so would prove a loss of time, for there existed no precedent whatever, that could bear upon the present case. The circumstances to be provided for did not depend upon their deliberations as a House of Parliament; it rested elsewhere. There was then a person in the kingdom differing from any other person that any existing precedents could refer to—an heir apparent of full age and capacity to exercise the royal power. It behoved them, therefore, to waste not a moment unnecessarily, but to proceed with all becoming diligence to restore the sovereign power and the exercise of the royal authority. . . . In his firm opinion, his royal highness the Prince of Wales had as clear, as express a right to assume the reins of government, and exercise the power of the sovereignty, during the continuance of the illness and incapacity with which it had pleased God to afflict his Majesty, as in the case of his Majesty's having undergone a natural and perfect demise. . . .

This unhappy intervention, on 10 December 1788, threw his own party into confusion. Grey and Sheridan, neither of whom had had prior warning of what Fox was going to say, upbraided him as they left the House after the debate, but for the sake of appearances they decided to support him in any future discussion of the question.

Pitt had slapped his thigh in jubilation, vowing that he would unwhig the gentleman for life, and in his reply he exploited his rival's error of judgment:

> If a claim of right is intimated (even though not formally) on the part of the Prince of Wales, to assume the government, it became of the utmost consequence, to ascertain, from precedent and history, whether this claim was founded; which, if it was, precluded the House from the possibility of all deliberation on the subject. In the meantime, he maintained . . . that to assert such a right in the Prince of Wales, or anyone else, independent of the decision of the two Houses of Parliament, was little less than treason to the constitution of the country. . . . (I)n the case of the interruption of the personal exercise of the royal authority, without any previous lawful provision having been made for carrying on the government, it belonged to the other branches of the legislature, on the part of the nation at large . . . to provide, according to their discretion, for the temporary exercise of the royal authority, in the name, and on the behalf of the sovereign, in such manner as they shall think requisite. . . .

Fox had made further discussion of the 'abstract' issue inevitable, and instead of shortening the proceedings his speech prolonged them. While Pitt was master of his material, Fox understood the doctrine of inherent right imperfectly, and employed it carelessly. Pitt had studied precedent; Fox had not. Fox attempted to wriggle out of the consequences of his mistake by claiming that there was general agreement on the practical steps to be taken, and that no purpose could be served by debating the 'abstract' issue. He even resorted to the old excuse that he had been misrepresented, but this merely proved how haphazard his attitude to the point in dispute was; and when Sheridan, in an otherwise conciliatory speech on 12 December, hinted at the dangers of provoking the Prince to assert his right, the contrast between the advocates of the Prince's right and the defenders of Parliamentary privilege was indelibly printed on the public memory. Much has been made of the inversion of roles over the Regency, the whigs propounding a royalist thesis, the tories a Parliamentary one. But this makes the error of assuming that Pitt and his followers were tories, and that something approximating to the modern two-party system was in operation. It also ignores the unbalanced nature of the controversy. Whilst Pitt took the constitutional problem seriously, Fox never faced it squarely and certainly never understood it. The dispute was not over the person of the Regent, but over the mode of his appointment and the scope of his authority. Pitt had conceded the Prince's claim, but by insisting that Parliament retained the right to restrict the Regent's powers he foiled the whigs, who were relying on royal patronage to buttress their position.

Although North—now blind and virtually in retirement—was called forth to bring some welcome common sense and moderation to the opposition's case, Pitt pressed on unflinchingly. The highly technical controversy continued through December and January, into February; and as the ministry inflicted a series of defeats on the whigs, Pitt gained encouragement from Willis's reports of the King's steady progress, despite bitter wrangles between the doctors. Restrictions were to be imposed on the Regent which would make it impossible for the Prince to exploit his position on behalf of his friends, and whilst a flood of addresses from towns and boroughs throughout the country demonstrated the strength of popular support for Pitt, Fox, sad at heart and weakened by dysentery, took refuge at Bath. The whigs did little to counter the ministry's successes, but in the Commons one voice was raised in violent protest against Pitt's principles and policy. Burke— disgusted by the cowardice of his colleagues and outraged by Pitt's attack on the sacred principle of hereditary succession—argued the case for the Prince with uncompromising vehemence. Frequently called to order because of the extravagance of his accusations, his behaviour prompted many of his contemporaries to suspect that he was mentally deranged, and no one perceived the insight and consistency underlying his fury. However mistaken his interpretation of the constitutional situation, he had grasped the fact that a real problem existed, that the abstract issues were relevant, and that they could not be conjured away by Fox's blithe denials. He saw, too, that if the opposition challenged Pitt's claim that Parliament had the right to supply the exigency, a coherent interpretation would have to be submitted as an alternative to that so ably outlined by the minister. But his lonely rearguard action only emphasised how different Burke's conception of the crisis was from that of the majority of his associates. Only Loughborough had taken the technicalities of the Regency with equal seriousness, and his motives were more questionable. Burke knew that whatever the outcome of the struggle for power, he would not be given a Cabinet post, and his wife thought that he would be forgotten in the scramble for places. The Regency debates disclosed the gulf which separated Burke from the other whig leaders and prepared the way for the great schism over the French Revolution.

When the King recovered his senses at the end of February 1789, before the Regency Bill became law, the whigs were embittered, bewildered, and divided. Weaknesses, soon to prove fatal during the controversy over the French Revolution, had been ruthlessly exposed. Pitt, on the other hand, was more firmly established than ever, his opponents cowed and broken at the end of the greatest political crisis since 1784. Yet, if he had enjoyed good fortune he deserved to do so. His conduct had been dignified and responsible. He had defended the rights of the King and the privileges of Parliament, and, as a proud gesture of independence, he had refused the offer of £100,000 from the merchants of London. The King's recovery was celebrated with fireworks and bright lights and all the rowdy humour of eighteenth-century public occasions. Fresh from another triumph Pitt was free to continue his work of retrenchment and reform at home, and his peaceful, but resolute, policy abroad. But the cheers for the King had hardly died away when the States-General met at Versailles, and all Pitt's hopes were quenched by a tumult terrifying in its intensity. If the nation's financial stability was to be maintained, a period of low expenditure was needed, and for this reason alone Pitt was preoccupied with keeping the peace. He had no wish to intervene in France's domestic quarrels, however disturbing these might become. But he was to learn that impartiality was no safeguard against a revolution which increasingly assumed the proportions of a universal catastrophe, and in the struggle with the new order he could not remain uncommitted.

Yet, in the years of his peacetime ministry, he had achieved much. The restoration of public finance; the revival of British prestige; the reform of the customs; the Indian legislation; the encouragement of trade; all these more than offset the disappointments experienced over Parliamentary reform, the Slave Trade, and Ireland. On the eve of the great war with France, Pitt estimated a steady annual surplus of about half a million pounds, after £1,000,000 had been paid into the Sinking Fund. Eleven millions of the funded debt had been written off, and public confidence was so great that in March 1792 Consols stood at 97. It has often been regretted, by those lucky enough to enjoy the advantage of hindsight, that no more was accomplished. Pitt, allegedly absolute in politics and independent alike of King and Commons, has been accused of negligence, even of treachery, because he did not make Parliamentary reform and the abolition of the Slave Trade the subjects of official legislation.

But the facts contradict these assertions. Pitt could not afford to disregard either the will of the King, or the convictions of the average Member of Parliament, however unenlightened these appear to modern sensibilities. Despite the emphasis which has been placed on the 'popular' nature of Pitt's electoral victory in 1784, it remains true to say that he could not carry the Commons with him whenever he was manifestly ahead of public or Parliamentary opinion. In 1788, in a House of 558 members, only 52 were described as attached to Pitt, and of these it was calculated that no more than 20 would be returned in an election held when he was no longer minister. As against this 138 were set down as Fox's party, and for his majority Pitt relied on the party of the Crown, the supporters of any government 'not peculiarly unpopular', and on the independents. He had, therefore, to take care not to provoke the hostility of conservative Members of the House, most of whom adopted a safety first attitude towards reform, particularly if their own privileges and interests were involved. In circumstances like these it is nonsensical to condemn Pitt in terms appropriate only to a period when doctrines of Cabinet responsibility, and of the place of the Crown in politics, as well as the concept of party discipline, had reached something like their modern form. It was possible to procure the election of M.P.s: it was virtually impossible to exercise any regular discipline upon them once they had taken their seats. Many Members were slack in their attendance; even during the Regency Crisis, when a new government was in the offing, many Members preferred to stay at home, and in the weeks before Christmas many who had come up to London drifted homewards. If a Member changed sides in the House, the most that could be threatened was his replacement at the next election, but this was a crude and imprecise means of imposing discipline. In an age which treasured political individualism, and which insisted that there was a patriotic line of conduct which all men of goodwill were able to discern, any approximation to party discipline was distrusted as a repugnant symptom of political degeneration, of the corrupting influence of faction.

The magic wand of official legislation would have disintegrated in

Pitt's hand, had he attempted to force measures of reform upon the King and recalcitrant members of the Cabinet, and the consequence would have been the collapse of his administration. The main purpose of government was not to introduce programmes of legislation, backed by the machinery of party organisation and the three-line whip. Wellington's famous dictum, that the King's government must be carried on, voiced the practice of the eighteenth and early nineteenth centuries. Yet men were suspicious of the executive, and sought to limit its sphere of action. Bureaucratic interference was an affront to the traditional liberties of Englishmen, and was best kept to a minimum. Freedom was valued more highly than efficiency. The sessions of Parliament were shorter, and ministers were expected to deal with the problems of war, foreign affairs, and finance, as and when they arose. They had first to persuade Parliament of their competence to perform these tasks, and their relationship with it was very different from that of a twentieth-century Cabinet. And Pitt was content to accept the constitutional conventions of the day. He recognised the right of the King to choose his ministers; he denounced any attempt to impose a Cabinet on the King; he conceded the sovereign's right to veto legislation. For too long he has been depicted, either as a tory democrat, ruling as the representative of the King and the people (and, one might add, the City) in defiance of the whig aristocracy; or as a liberal, who, after a promising beginning, deserted the true cause in the 1790s. Both of these interpretations are far from the truth; both obscure the real nature of his achievement. Even more misleading is the sensational picture of the hypocrite who used the reform movement to establish his own power, only to betray it once it had served his purpose; of the meretricious politician who neglected, for selfish reasons of place and prestige, to reform abuses whilst there was still time. All of these misrepresentations arise from a determination to see Pitt as a modern prime minister, without placing him firmly in the context of eighteenth-century politics.

They are also founded on a false reading of his character. He was neither a cunning Machiavellian, indifferent to human feelings and exploiting them for his own ends; nor an icy superman, devoid of emotions and sympathy. His sheltered upbringing, and lifelong celibacy, have led to misconceptions. In an effort to master his shyness he adopted an aloof dignity in public. When he entered the Commons

he glanced neither to right nor to left, in stark contrast with Charles
Fox's bustling informality. But there were intense feelings behind the
glacial exterior. He rigorously restrained himself in public, but when
Dundas was disgraced in 1805 he broke down and wept in the House.
Yet, with a characteristic gesture, he pulled his hat over his face to hide
the tears which were streaming down his cheeks. In private life he
could relax, and tales were told of drunken jaunts with Dundas, including one in which the minister was shot at by an angry farmer. His
fondness for port wine—neatly summed up in Addington's remark
that if there was one thing Pitt liked better than a glass of port it was a
bottle—inspired many lampoons, the most famous being the couplet:

> Pitt: *I cannot see the Speaker, Hal, can you?*
> Dundas: *Not see the Speaker! Damme, I see two!*

His friends remembered him as a witty conversationalist, and a delightful companion. Richard Wellesley described his manners as 'perfectly
plain' and thought him 'endowed beyond any man of his time whom
I knew, with a gay heart and a social spirit'. He loved small dinner-
parties, with several close friends as his guests. His habits were as simple
as his manners. He breakfasted punctually at nine, and often used the
meal to entertain visitors. He rarely took a holiday, but from time to
time he went to Brighton, to Burton Pynsent, and to Wilberforce's
villa at Wimbledon. At week-ends he retired to Holwood or Walmer
Castle. For exercise he went out riding. He liked the company of
young people and on one occasion he allowed the Stanhope and
Napier children to blacken his face with cork, during a boisterous
romp. When Hawkesbury and Castlereagh called unexpectedly he
soon recovered his usual dignity, but the game was resumed once they
had gone. He read the classics at every opportunity, and although his
acquaintance with contemporary literature was slight he praised Robert
Burns to Lord Aberdeen. In religious matters he was a dutiful member
of the Church of England. When the Protestant Dissenters petitioned
for the repeal of the Test and Corporation Acts, he followed the advice
of the Bishops in rejecting the demand. He distrusted religious enthusiasm, interpreting Christianity as a guide to conduct, rather than an
intense personal experience. He viewed religious dogma with some
scepticism, and his comment to Wilberforce, that Butler's *Analogy*
raised more problems than it solved, suggests that he thought critically

about accepted modes of belief. On his death-bed he professed faith in Christ, but it does not seem that religious convictions played any dominant part in determining his outlook and behaviour.

Ironically the guardian of the nation's finances was incapable of looking after his own affairs. He carelessly acquired new liabilities, and was often ignorant of the true state of his finances, but there is no adequate explanation of the anxiety which pursued him throughout his career. Several factors contributed to his embarrassment. He was kind to his mother, and generous to his brother. He was persistently defrauded by unscrupulous tradesmen. His butcher, his tailor, his wine-merchant, all charged fantastic sums to his account. Goods were delivered without being ordered, and in quantities far in excess of his wants, and the prices in every case were grotesquely inflated. In 1785 Pitt bought Holwood Hill—'a most beautiful spot, wanting nothing but a house fit to live in'. He could not really afford to do so, and the improvements he made on the estate, together with his experiments in landscape gardening, meant that the charming residence was a constant drain on his already overtaxed resources. Despite the efforts of his friends, and occasional attempts to set his house in order, he never supervised his expenditure with sufficient attention, and throughout his years in office he was never free from the importunate demands of creditors, many of whom ruthlessly exploited his negligence.

Pitt's ascendancy in the Commons was undoubted. His gifts were equalled, but not surpassed, by the galaxy of debating talent on the opposition benches. His intellectual pre-eminence within the Cabinet was assured. But he had to deal with men who were as determined to uphold their opinions as they were willing to voice them. Relations within the Cabinet often influenced policy. Pitt had to humour Thurlow, the King's nominee as Lord Chancellor, and until he dismissed the unreliable and surly lawyer in 1792, he had to face his obstructive tactics on many occasions. Although Pitt was close to Dundas, that skilled and experienced administrator did not always share his progressive views, and his cousin, William Wyndham Grenville, was dour and unimaginative, as well as loyal and industrious. Others, like Sydney and Leeds, needed careful handling, and, whatever his virtues, Pitt was not at his best in smoothing over personal antagonisms and rivalries. The sarcasm which he used so devastatingly in debate was a less happy instrument in more intimate discussion, and his inability to suffer fools gladly made him an exacting and unyielding master. He did not trouble to disguise his contempt for much of the place hunting and jobbery which were so important a part of the contemporary scene, and his frequent use of the peerage as a means of rewarding political services earned him much criticism. Like so many great men, he knew loneliness, and this was intensified after the death of his favourite sister, Harriet Eliot, in 1786.

But he had soon to brace himself to face new trials, of an order which he had not yet experienced. In France the situation was deteriorating. The government's attempts at reform were foiled. Financial collapse loomed ever nearer. The States-General, in abeyance since 1614, were called to deal with the multitudinous problems weighing down Louis XVI's doomed government. But, when the representatives of the three estates met in May 1789 the King's failure to take the initiative heightened the determination of the third estate to speak for the nation. Disorder in Paris and the provinces, the shortage of bread, suspicions of the King's good faith, rumours of a military coup, and strange tales of organised brigandage—all found their culmination in the sack of the Bastille, an almost empty relic of a bygone era, containing a few lunatics and criminals, and garrisoned by a handful of pensioners, but a symbol, nevertheless, of all that was hated and feared. Privilege was questioned, attacked, and abolished, with all the deceptive ease of debate, the nobility (so lately the stubborn defenders of their antique rights) co-operating with an enthusiasm compounded of anxiety and hope. A legal revolution had been accomplished, the protest of a class against an outmoded social structure. When Price and Burke raised their voices in a controversy which was to echo down the years, Pitt could no longer ignore events in France, however much he sought to content himself with a few safe platitudes. Almost four years separated the meeting of the States-General from the outbreak of war, but the years of peace were over: the conflict with the revolution had begun.

4 THE FRENCH REVOLUTION AND WAR, 1789-1801

DURING the early months of the French Revolution the collapse of the Old Order, and the breakdown of government, were watched with fascinated horror or animated approval by Englishmen who had little understanding of the issues at stake in the struggle between the King of France and the National Assembly. Ignorance of French conditions was widespread, and the temptation to see the revolution purely in terms of English experience was irresistible. Some observers were sympathetic, even enthusiastic: others were bored, indifferent, or sardonically patronising. The French were at last emulating the Glorious Revolution of 1688, and, if they had taken a hundred years to profit from that enlightened example, the establishment of liberty on the English model seemed the inevitable culmination of that Anglo-mania which had been so fashionable amongst French intellectuals. Dissenting ministers, already pressing for the repeal of the Test and Corporation Acts as the most fitting commemoration of William III's landing at Torbay, hailed the meeting of the States-General as another milestone on the road to civil and religious liberty: Calvinistic sobriety had given way to Unitarian optimism. Charles Fox, convinced that the real danger to the constitution lay in the growth of 'tory principles', thought that what was happening in France was 'likely to be useful . . . in keeping alive and invigorating the spirit of liberty', and he imme-diately identified the revolution with the cause dearest to his heart —the unending battle against the power of the Crown. This, rather than any profound insight, inspired his famous outburst on hearing of the fall of the Bastille, 'How much the greatest event that has happened in the history of the world, and how much the best!' Samuel Romilly rejoiced at the revolution. Major Cartwright affirmed that the French were advancing the liberties of mankind. Even Hannah More exulted in the demolition of the Bastille, confessing (somewhat rhetorically) several years later: 'What lover of his species did not triumph in the warm hope that one of the finest countries in the world would soon be one of the most free?'

But there were other attitudes, less zealous, more typically insular. Many Englishmen remembered with indignation and shame the assistance given by the French monarchy to the American rebels during their fight for independence, and the humiliations now inflicted on Louis XVI seemed a just retribution for Yorktown and the loss of the thirteen colonies. The ancient enemy was paying the price for her folly in embarking on a war which she could not afford, and in defence of principles which questioned the authority of legally constituted government. Crippled by internal strife, she would cease to be a threat to the balance of power in Europe: perhaps she would also decline as a commercial rival. There was little apprehension of the challenge made by the revolution to ordered society and traditional forms of government throughout the Continent. The ideas of 1789 were not yet exported in soldiers' knapsacks or expounded by terror, and, despite all the bold talk about the rights of man, the republican party within the National Assembly was an insignificant minority. Edmund Burke brooded darkly over the chaos which was engulfing the heritage of the Bourbons, but his warnings of the wrath to come—however justified by subsequent events—were out of harmony with the feelings general in those warm summer days, when to be young was 'very heaven', and 'the whole earth the beauty wore of paradise'. Burke's pessimism only earned him the impatient scorn of those reasonable men who confidently expected the birth of a golden age, and who trusted the essential goodness of human nature. The legend of Edmund the Jesuit died hard, and Burke was described by his most faithful disciple as 'a man decried, persecuted, and proscribed; not being much valued, even by his own party, and by half the nation considered as little better than an ingenious madman'. Meanwhile the enlightened hastened to their own destiny.

Pitt regarded the proceedings at Versailles with cool detachment. He had no wish to meddle in the internal affairs of the most powerful State in Europe. Peace was his primary aim, for he needed a period of stability to reap the benefits of his fiscal policies. War was an expensive and dangerous luxury. He sympathised with the creation of a moderate, constitutional monarchy in France, but he hated mob rule and incitements to violence, and the condonation of bloodshed by those responsible for the maintenance of law and order. For him, as for most Englishmen, the mob was associated with the ferocities of the Gordon riots. He had no patience with the special pleading of Barnave: to ask 'Was the blood that was shed so very pure?' did not lessen the enormity of the crime. Even before the fall of the Bastille, he told his mother that the French were

> coming to actual extremes, the King having suddenly dismissed M. Necker, and appearing determined to support his authority against the National Assembly. This scene, added to the prevailing scarcity, makes that country an object of compassion even to a rival.

As long as the conflict that was raging in France affected no other country, Pitt was determined to take no action. During the Nootka Sound crisis in 1790 he insisted that

> no assurances shall be given, directly or indirectly, which go farther than that this country means to preserve in the neutrality which it has hitherto scrupulously observed with respect to the internal dissensions of France.

He wanted to cultivate friendly relations between the two countries, but he was cautious about any formal alliance, for changing circumstances might make it inadvisable, even impossible, to meet such a commitment. It was necessary to exercise the utmost care to avoid giving the impression that the British government favoured any one of the French political parties. Pitt had no interest in schemes to restore the authority of the King of France. A monarchical crusade made no appeal to his severely practical mind, and he took no part in ill-starred gestures like the Declaration of Pillnitz, which discredited the royalist cause and encouraged suspicions of Louis XVI's good faith. Nor did he share Burke's enthusiasm for the émigrés. The court at Coblentz, with its empty sabre rattling and impotent arrogance, was as repugnant as the extremist factions within the assembly. Like many others, he thought Burke's denunciation of the revolution exaggerated, if not unfounded, and the latter's obsession with French affairs seemed an embarrassing lapse of taste. Pitt's political experience, and keen appreciation of the realities of public life, made him distrust facile generalisations and gay optimism, but he was equally incapable of following the broad sweeps of Burke's imagination. And, at this time, Burke's behaviour was as exasperating to his friends as it was bewildering to his enemies. Even the Duke of Portland, who got on well with Burke personally, found it impossible to invite him to dinner without running the risk of a harangue on the evils of the French Revolution. Pitt shared this perplexity. During one dinner-party in Burke's company in 1791, he could not refrain from commenting, after a long sally about the French fashion in politics, 'Depend upon it, Mr. Burke, we shall go on as we are until the Day of Judgment.' 'Very likely, sir,' was the reply, 'it is the day of no judgment I am afraid of!' For Burke in his turn, found the minister's moderation reprehensible. Pitt and Grenville were 'right in their general inclination', but when it came to practical action against the revolution, they were 'cold and dead'.

His own reaction was vehement. He made his distrust of the revolution plain in several speeches in the Commons, and in November 1790 he published his *Reflections on the Revolution in France*, ostensibly written to a young member of the French National Assembly, and intended as a reply to a sermon preached by the Unitarian minister, the Reverend Richard Price. Burke brought passion and poetry, imagination and insight, to a problem beset by superficial generalisations. Ill-informed on the structure of French society, ignorant of the fundamental causes of the revolution, obsessed with the idea of a plot against society, and too willing to interpret the Old Order in France in terms of the British constitution, he nevertheless perceived that the revolution threatened the assumptions underlying eighteenth-century civilisation, realising, before many of the revolutionaries themselves were aware of their missionary vocation, that it was an international phenomenon. With his deep sense of history, his reverence for tradition, his contempt for mere reason, and his concern for morality, he brought a religious intensity to his study of the French catastrophe. The wisdom of the past was jeopardised by the shallow deceptions of rationalist thought: theoretical definitions of liberty only imperilled real freedom. Abstract propositions, divorced from the situation in which they were to be applied, were irreparable delusions.

> Circumstances [he wrote] . . . give in reality to every political principle its distinguishing colour and discriminating effect. The circumstances are what render every civil and political scheme beneficial or noxious to mankind. . . . Is it because liberty in the abstract may be classed amongst the blessings of mankind, that I am seriously to felicitate a madman who has escaped from the protecting restraint and darkness of his cell, on his restoration to the enjoyment of light and liberty?

He proposed to suspend his judgment on 'French liberty' until he knew

> how it had been combined with government; with public force; with the discipline and obedience of armies; with the collection of an effective and well distributed revenue; with morality and religion; with the solidity of property; with peace and order; with civil and social manners.

Society was a living organism, to be looked upon with veneration. It could not be dissolved 'by the fancy of parties'. Rather it was a 'partnership in all science; a partnership in all art; a partnership in every virtue and in all perfection'. In prose of great power and grandeur he expounded a doctrine of government which transcended mere tracts for the times. Handicapped by his deficient and often inaccurate information on French affairs, and partially blinded by his own prejudices, he nevertheless swooped with the insight of genius on the tragic flaw underlying the hopes of Price and the revolutionaries alike: humanity was imperfect. Government was no magic solution for men's ills, nor was it dependent on so-called natural rights. It was 'a contrivance of human wisdom to provide for human wants', 'a consideration of convenience', and its exercise called for a profound knowledge of human nature and 'the most delicate and complicated skill'. Even the most laudable schemes could have lamentable consequences. Despite all the talk of the will of the people, there was no means of ensuring that the new régime—its power unlimited and uncontrolled—would prove a better master than the old. Burke demanded practical safeguards for liberty and definite assurances that the business of government could be carried on. With uncanny foresight he predicted that the corruptions of power would lead to terror, to bloody anarchy, to

civil war, and finally to military dictatorship. He exposed the inexperience of the men in whose hands the destiny of France was placed, and
laid bare their true motives, in which disinterested idealism was mingled
with class envy, the remembrance of past wrongs, and the desire to
destroy.

The imaginative appeal made by the tragedy encompassing the
representatives of ancient dynasties led his generous spirit to indulge
in excesses (he had never been famous for moderation), and in fanciful
bursts of rhetoric such as the famous passage extolling the beauty of
Marie Antoinette. However much he merited the down-to-earth
criticism of Tom Paine—'Mr. Burke pities the plumage but forgets
the dying bird'—it was precisely this aspect of his thought which made
the greatest impression on contemporaries. In the fury of controversy
men ignored those themes which had been constant throughout
Burke's career. He was welcomed as a convert to toryism, and hailed
as the eloquent defender of the *status quo*. George III paid the *Reflections*
the dubious compliment of saying that every gentleman ought to read
them. On the other side their author was reviled as a renegade. But he
was no apostate, and rightly claimed that his differences with the whigs
turned on no trivial issues. His concern for the hereditary succession
had long been evident, and during the Regency crisis he had defended
the right of the Prince of Wales to assume the royal authority on the
same grounds which now led him to denounce the revolution in
France. He was still preoccupied with the preservation of the British
constitution, and the protection of the real liberties enjoyed by the
subjects of King George. Indeed, it can be argued that his primary
purpose was to forestall any repercussions in England—'Whenever our
neighbour's house is on fire, it cannot be amiss for the engines to play
a little on our own.' The acclaim which greeted the *Reflections* was the
climax to a life haunted by irony. Many of those who echoed and
cheapened Burke's ideas had been only too glad, in the not so distant
past, to sneer at him as an Irish adventurer. Oblivious to the profundi-
ties of his thought, and to the full meaning of his positive concept of
society, they used his great name to cloak their own intellectual
bankruptcy. To the end of his life Burke was misunderstood, misrepresented, and cruelly abused.

Burke's onslaught provoked a counter-attack, and many regretted
that a public controversy had been precipitated when the most popular,

and in many ways the most able, reply was Tom Paine's *The Rights of Man*, the first part of which was published in March 1791, the second part—regarded as much more dangerous by the authorities—coming out in February 1792. Paine, with all the wisdom of an uncommon 'common man', coolly revealed the weakness of Burke's appeal to the past—the implication that the living were bound by the decisions of the dead:

> Every age and generation must be free to act for itself in all cases as the ages and generations which preceded it. The vanity and presumption of governing beyond the grave is the most ridiculous and insolent of all tyrannies.

He also showed that Burke was ignorant of the underlying causes of the revolution, for the nation had risen, not against the inoffensive Louis XVI, but 'against the despotic principles of government'. Burke had deplored the savagery with which the populace had wreaked vengeance upon its victims, but that ferocity was itself the product of the tyrannical oppression under which the people of France had lived. Nor was it just to lay the outrages of the 'mob' to the charge of the whole people: Paine was very much a man of his time, and insisted on making a distinction between the two. In his defence of the new French constitution, he criticised the abuses of the English Parliament —the unequal distribution of Parliamentary seats, the vagaries of the franchise, the corruptions of electoral influence. He affirmed the rights of man and the sovereignty of the people—doctrines which became tainted with suspicions of Jacobinism after the outbreak of war—but he thought of society in individualistic terms. He shared that distrust of administrative interference so popular amongst country gentlemen in the eighteenth century, and he had a deep-rooted dislike of all governments:

> Formal Government makes but a small part of civilised life. . . . It is to the great and fundamental principles of society and civilisation . . . infinitely more than to anything which even the best instituted Government can perform, that the safety and prosperity of the individual and of the whole depends. The more perfect civilisation is, the less occasion has it for Government, because the more does it regulate its own affairs and govern itself.

He put his finger on the contradiction inherent in Burke's attitude to the revolution of 1688. If that revolution was justified, why was it argued that no similar necessity could arise, in different circumstances, at a later stage of historical development?

> The Parliament or the people of 1688 or any other period had no more right to dispose of the people of the present day . . . than the Parliament or the people of the present day have to dispose of, bind, or controul those who are to live a hundred or two thousand years hence. Every generation is, and must be, competent to all the purposes which its occasions require. . . .

Yet, for all the contrast between their characters, careers, and intellectual positions, Burke and Paine were both justified by the situation in which they were writing. Burke sensed the dangers of defying tradition, of relying on the reasonableness of human nature, of invoking abstract rights without a sufficient knowledge of the facts: Paine was aware of the folly of allowing reverence for the past to become an idol: tradition had too often been invoked to disguise blind devotion to things as they were. Paine had a better understanding of the injustices of the Old Order, but, partly because he thought of the French Revolution principally in terms of the American, he was too optimistic in his hopes of a new world, and his expectations proved as ill-founded as Burke's apologia for the French constitution under the *ancien régime*. The Irishman's pessimism made him a wiser prophet.

It was not surprising that Burke's opinions led to the break-up of the old Rockingham party. It was not the first time that there had been differences of opinion, but on previous occasions—whether over the Prince of Wales's debts, Parliamentary reform, or the Regency—it had been possible to avoid an irreconcilable split, though this had been achieved partly at the cost of political effectiveness. But the issues were now too great to be skimmed over, and Burke's denunciations threw Fox's cheerful enthusiasm into greater relief. But even Fox was not without moments of uncertainty: on one occasion he commented, 'Well, Burke is right, but he is right too soon.' Burke went so far as to claim that 'inwardly Fox did not differ from me materially if at all', but, once the controversy had become public, and especially when suggestions were made that a coalition with Pitt might ensue, attitudes stiffened. There was no way of reconciling positions which were held with obstinate devotion on both sides. The behaviour of Fox and Burke in the Commons indicated an appreciable divergence of views. Nevertheless, attempts were made to reach a compromise, and on 21 April 1791 the two old campaigners went down to the debate on the Quebec Bill arm in arm. But it was for the last time. The discussion of the new constitution for Canada soon led to references to the constitution-making which was going on in Paris. When the debate was resumed on 6 May, Burke, stung by gibes which he considered as a series of deliberate insults, attacked the French Revolution, as different from the English as 'wisdom from folly, as virtue from vice, as the most opposite extremes in nature'. Fox tried to soothe the affront, possibly because he felt that Burke had been unduly provoked. He sought to characterise the difference of opinion as only a disagreement on points of theory, rather than practical politics. But he ruined everything by referring to the French Revolution as one of the most glorious events in the history of mankind, and Burke was compelled to answer. He condemned the fashionable practice of praising the French Revolution at the expense of the English, and however indiscreet it might be at his time of life to offend friends, his love of the British constitution, as well as duty and prudence, taught him to exclaim, with his last words, 'Fly from the French Constitution!' At this moment Fox interrupted, whispering, 'There is no loss of friends', but Burke was immune to all personal loyalties. 'Yes!' he burst out, 'there is loss of friends—he knew the price of his conduct—he had done his duty at the price of his friend—their friendship was at an end!' Silence fell upon the House. Fox rose to reply, but, in the sober language of the *Parliamentary History*,

> his mind was so much agitated, and his heart so much affected by what had fallen from Mr. Burke, that it was some minutes before he could proceed. Tears trickled down his cheeks, and he strove in vain to give utterance to the feelings that dignified and exalted his nature. The sensibility of every member of the House appeared uncommonly excited upon the occasion.

Fox sobbed uncontrollably in his grief: he could not comprehend why a political dispute should sever old ties of affection and regard. When he recovered his self-possession he paid an eloquent tribute to his old colleague, but their friendship was no more. Six years later, when Fox tried to visit Burke on his death-bed, he was turned away.

It is worth recalling that the intimacy of their friendship has been exaggerated. Burke had never belonged to the inner circle of Fox's friends, and his isolation within the opposition had become more pronounced with every year that had passed since Rockingham's death. His habit of seeing political issues in terms of truth and falsehood often embarrassed his associates, who showed the impatience of men of the world when confronted with an intellectual in politics, and they never understood the ideas which he expounded with such vehemence and at great length. His speeches, despite his posthumous reputation as an orator, were overloaded with learning. The refinements of his thought were far above the heads of his audience, and only made weary country gentlemen sigh for the dinner-bell. He urged moderation in the management of public affairs, but displayed little of that quality in the House, for his passionate temperament made it impossible for him to discuss any matter of national concern without betraying the deepest, and often the most violent, feelings. Many of the whigs never forgot that Burke's father had been an Irish attorney, and that he himself was surrounded by shady relatives who had been implicated in doubtful financial speculations. Even his intense devotion to close friends seemed wrong-headed, and, on occasion, suspicious. But, whatever they thought of Burke, the whig aristocrats found it difficult to take Fox's part over the French Revolution. Baffled by Burke's metaphysics, they were none the less wary of Fox's defence of the principles of 1789, realising that these were antagonistic to their place in society and in politics: the revolution demanded other credentials for office than high birth and social prestige. But, as yet, the bond of friendship was stronger than the dictates of political wisdom. Perhaps the affair would blow over, as so many others had done, without dividing the party irrevocably.

Pitt took little interest in the intellectual debate. Although he saw the increasing embarrassment of the opposition with some relief, he was preoccupied with the tasks of executive government, pressing on with his financial measures and introducing legislation to deal with the situation in Canada. Here he had to pay one of the legacies of the American War. Despite Shelburne's pledges on compensation, the thorny question of the American loyalists had never been settled, and many of these unfortunates, denounced as traitors by those whom they themselves regarded as lucky rebels, and forgotten by the government to which they had remained faithful at no small cost, had emigrated to Canada. But the influx of English-speaking Protestants created new problems in a colony which, despite the transfer of sovereignty in 1763, had remained predominantly French and Catholic. Pitt divided the country into two provinces—Upper and Lower Canada, in an endeavour to secure justice for both groups. He defended this decision in the Commons' debates on the Canada Bill:

> . . . If the province were not to be divided, there would be only one House of Assembly; and there being two parties, if these parties had been equal, or nearly equal, in the Assembly, it would have been the source of perpetual faction; while, if one party had been much stronger than the other, the minority might, not without some justice, call itself oppressed.

Pitt's aim was to

> put an end to the differences of opinion and growing competition between the ancient inhabitants, and the new settlers from England and America . . . and to bring the government of the province as near as the nature and situation of it would admit to the British Constitution.

There were to be elected assemblies in both provinces, as well as nominated legislative and executive councils, but the responsibility for executive decisions still lay with the Governor. The Act had weaknesses: the British minority in Lower Canada felt that they had been abandoned, whilst those in Upper Canada resented customs duties imposed at Quebec. But, though Pitt had not granted fully responsible government, he had at least opened the way to establishing elected assemblies, and the division of the country was a reasonable means of softening bitter feeling between French and British Canadians. At the same time, whatever its merits, Pitt's legislation was based, not on any imperial vision, but on a bleak examination of the facts. His attitude to the settlement of Botany Bay and the transportation of convicts to Australia also emphasises his indifference towards concepts of empire. Transportation was the cheapest method of disposing of convicts, and Australia was the most distant spot to which they could be sent. But it would be absurd to berate Pitt for not being an imperialist. Like all those who had lived through the American War he was cautious and sceptical when dealing with colonial matters, and he preferred to avoid trouble rather than to blaze new trails. The reorganisation of Canada was necessary because discontent might lead to another outbreak of colonial disaffection. Australia was merely a strange, undeveloped, mysterious continent: no dreams of grandeur disturbed the minister's calm practicality.

While the French monarchy staggered on towards dissolution, Britain became involved in disputes with two other powers, Spain and Russia. Although now in decline, Spain still claimed the western coast of America from Cape Horn to Alaska, and, however much doughty mariners might ignore, or even despise, this obsolete and illusory dominion, his Catholic Majesty resented illegal trespass by interlopers and vagabonds. The British had been particularly offensive in this respect, and when in 1790 several British vessels were apprehended off Vancouver Island, where there was a small British settlement at Nootka, memories of Jenkins' Ear were stirred by tales of crews in irons and stories of Spanish arrogance. Pitt pressed for satisfaction. Parliament, enthusiastic in defence of national interests, voted a million pounds for the fleet, and tempers were roused by the knowledge that the captured sailors had been released only because of their presumed ignorance of their offence. The old claim was still urged in full force. The situation was further complicated by the ambiguous attitude of the French: did they consider themselves bound by the family compact with Spain? Happily for Britain the National Assembly used the crisis to undermine the powers of the Crown, and the agreement between the two branches of the House of Bourbon was denounced as a basis for French foreign policy. Meanwhile Holland and Prussia avowed their willingness to stand by their obligations under the Triple Alliance, and a British fleet was prepared to give added force to verbal protests. The Spaniards sensed their impotence and isolation and gave way. British merchants were allowed to establish trading posts on the western coast of the American continent, on the understanding that they did not come within ten leagues of any Spanish settlement, that business was carried on in a peaceful manner, and that no illicit trade took place with the Spanish colonies.

Pitt was less successful when he intervened in the affairs of eastern Europe. Britain's sea power was of little utility without the support of the Prussian army, and though Frederick William was disturbed by the conduct of Catherine the Great, his suspicions of the Austrian Emperor, and his own designs on Poland, made him change his attitude. In the late 1780s Catherine was pursuing an aggressive policy against the Ottoman Empire, and Joseph II of Austria also seized the opportunity of attacking the Sultan. The critical situation in the Balkans had been one of the reasons why the French had given way to the British and Prussians in the Netherlands, and in 1788 the Triple Alliance had compelled the Danes to come to terms with the Swedes, who had made the most of the Russian Empress's preoccupation with

Turkey by attacking her forces in Finland—with catastrophic results, for the Russian navy defeated the Swedish fleet at Sveaborg. But, though the King of Sweden made peace with Russia, the war against the Turks continued. Belgrade fell to the Austrians; Bucharest to the Russians. But the death of Joseph II transformed the balance of power, for his brother, Leopold, sought to end the adventurous and dangerous foreign policy. Peace was made with the Sultan on the basis of the *status quo*. Catherine II, however, ignored suggestions that she, too, should come to terms. She saw no reason for halting the advance of her victorious armies, or for abandoning her policy of expansion towards the Black Sea.

The King of Prussia, who believed that the Austrians would not help Catherine if she continued hostilities against Turkey, asked Britain to 'consider whether the best course of action would not be that of inducing Russia . . . to follow the example of the Emperor'. He suggested the cession of Orchakov, a fortress which the Russians had occupied and which gave them a superiority over the Turks 'which may be very prejudicial to the interests even of England'. The decisive moment was drawing near, and Frederick William wanted 'a definite declaration on this subject'. British opinion was divided. The Duke of Richmond disapproved of any pledge to go to war with Russia. The Duke of Leeds, on the other hand, called for a firm, truculent policy; he was determined to preserve the Triple Alliance, and was therefore prepared to act in accordance with Prussian wishes. An ultimatum was drafted, threatening British intervention if the Russian Empress did not return Orchakov to the Sultan. Fortunately it was never delivered. The Prussians were now less sure of Austrian support, and it soon became clear that Frederick William was more interested in acquiring new slices of Polish territory than in fighting for an obscure town on the Black Sea. Perhaps the three powers could settle their differences amicably, with the unhappy Poles providing compensation for all three. There was, in fact, no identity of interest between Prussia and Britain in eastern Europe. When it came to partitions of Poland Britain was irrelevant. The alliance had been born out of a mutual desire to keep the French out of the Low Countries: it was effective only in the west.

Pitt was willing to step down if a satisfactory method of saving face could be found. Less tenacious than Leeds, he was more sensitive to criticism. Without Prussia it was impossible to bring pressure to bear upon Russia, and, while Leeds talked of the need to save the Triple Alliance, Pitt was acutely conscious of its limitations. There was nothing to be gained by becoming involved in struggles in eastern Europe, and the civil confusions in France added another unpredictable element to an already bewildering situation. He was also aware of his weakness in the House of Commons on the Orchakov issue. Fox had attacked a war 'for the recovery of a single town', whilst Burke had maintained that any Christian power was to be preferred to 'those destructive savages', the Turks. Pitt's handling of the debates had been tactless. Embarrassed by divisions within the Cabinet, and uncertain of his ally's intentions, he had refused demands for information. Nor were financial considerations far from his mind: he doubted whether he would be able to carry the vote of credit, the House being unconscious of the 'most valuable interests of the country'. However sincere his own apprehensions were about Russian expansion towards the Mediterranean, however dangerous any alteration in the balance of power in the Near East would be, it would be folly to risk a breach with Prussia over the Balkans, or to involve the country in a war which it was ill-fitted to wage. Leeds thought that Pitt was weakly deserting his allies, that he was refusing to accept the necessary consequences of his policy. When Pitt sent a more conciliatory message to Catherine, conceding her right to keep Orchakov, Leeds resigned in protest, Grenville replacing him as Foreign Secretary. Four months later peace was signed between Russia and Turkey (August 1791).

Unlike Leeds, Pitt saw the gulf separating the objects of British policy in the Near East from their realisation, and he did not forget that wars cost money. But at the same time he was bitterly hurt by the failure over Orchakov. With tears in his eyes he told Ewart that it was the greatest mortification he had ever experienced, and he urged the ambassador to tell Frederick William 'of the real state of the business and the true motives of our conduct'. To persist in the Orchakov affair would have risked

> the existence of the present Government, and with it the whole of our system at home and abroad. . . . It is not difficult to foresee what must have been the consequence to Prussia of a change effected by an opposition to the very measures taken with that court and resting on the avowed ground of the present system of alliance.

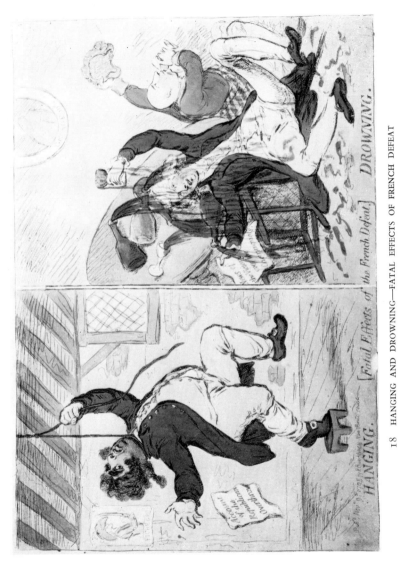

18 HANGING AND DROWNING—FATAL EFFECTS OF FRENCH DEFEAT

(While Fox hangs himself, Pitt and Dundas drown themselves in port)

From a caricature by James Gillray, 1795

19 CHARLES JAMES FOX
From the portrait by K. A. Hickel

But Pitt must have known that the fickle conduct of the Prussians was the main reason for his change of plan, and the knowledge that he had mishandled the business rankled in his mind. It is an exaggeration to talk about the collapse of Pitt's foreign policy, and inappropriate to suggest that he was, in any sense, required to resign, but he had sustained a severe reverse, and the knowledge that Fox's bust occupied a place of honour in the Russian Empress's drawing-room only made the experience all the more galling.

But new developments soon cast Orchakov into oblivion. In the west Austria and Prussia watched events in France with mounting concern. In the east Prussia, Russia, and Austria discovered a common interest in the dismemberment of Poland. The Kings of Europe made a poor showing in defence of the rights of crowned heads: they were more sensitive to the prospect of new territories, than anxious for the fate of the French monarchy. And the failure of the flight to Varennes revealed Louis XVI's plight in all its degradation. Though the National Assembly took refuge in verbal evasions, the attempted escape of the royal family, with its appeal to foreign powers to restore absolute monarchy in France, indicated the deep reluctance with which the new constitution had been accepted by the King, and exposed the sinister influence wielded by Marie Antoinette over her dull consort. Constitutional monarchy was discredited: the people had lost faith in their King. The nationalisation of the Church had ranged Louis's conscience against the revolution, and had introduced the incalculable religious element into a situation already charged with tension. Mirabeau had pleaded the cause of monarchy and Parliamentary government, but, though he was paid for his services by the King, his advice was ignored. In any case, his plans were fraught with danger: he had been willing to hazard, if not to precipitate, civil war, and his death quenched the last, faint hope for the reformed monarchy as envisaged by the constitutionalists of 1789.

After Varennes the King resorted to clumsy pieces of dishonesty in an effort to preserve his rights, but he had forfeited the loyalty of his subjects. When the National Assembly disbanded and the new Legislative Assembly met, moderate royalists were replaced by idealistic republicans, whose heads were full of romantic notions about the city-states of the ancient world. A self-denying ordinance prevented those who had sat in the previous assembly from enjoying membership of the new, and a mistaken application of the doctrine of the separation of the powers excluded executive ministers from the chamber. Men lacking political experience did not realise the strength of the passions they sought to rouse, and, whilst the Queen hoped to restore order with the help of foreign bayonets, the Girondins planned to secure their own triumph by waging war. Both expected to turn a national emergency to their own account. Robespierre, fearful lest the reactionaries should sweep to Paris and undo all that the revolution had accomplished, denounced the war policy of Brissot, but the Girondins had their way, and in the spring of 1792 France declared war on Austria. Prussia, who had made an Alliance with Austria in February, formally entered the war in July.

But the party which benefited most from the hostilities was that which had opposed them. The Jacobins soon proved that they were the only men capable of fighting the war and of saving the revolution. The French army had been weakened by the emigration of many of its officers, and by indiscipline amongst the troops, and after several humiliating defeats panic reigned in Paris, where ferocious patriots talked wildly of treachery and betrayal. On 10 August the monarchy was overthrown, and the King—suspected by many of treason—was suspended. A month later a republic was proclaimed, but, though Louis XVI became Citizen Capet, Brunswick's army marched on. Verdun fell to the Prussians. The Parisian mob yelled for the blood of traitors, and the September massacres gave them ample satisfaction, while enabling the Jacobins to win the elections as the party of national salvation. The Girondins, accused of betraying their country, shared the fate of the monarchy they had done so much to destroy. Danton, shrieking defiance at the coalesced Kings of Europe, emerged as the representative of the republic's will to survive, and at Valmy, in a battle fought with strange hesitancy on both sides, Goethe discerned the birth of a new era. Brunswick's advance was halted: the revolutionary levies had stemmed the legendary Prussian brigades. The Convention, dominated by the Mountain, crushed all resistance at home, and prepared to carry the ideals of the revolution abroad. The Decrees of November and December, disguised as professions of fraternity, promised aid to any people striving to throw off the yoke of a tyrant, and Britain heard the freedom of the Scheldt asserted by a power which had recognised Dutch control of the river in five treaties since

1713. In November, with the defeat of the Austrian army at Jemappes, the revolutionary columns poured into the Low Countries, and at the end of the month Antwerp fell. The Dutch now felt themselves threatened by an invigorated France, which seemed to possess unbounded confidence and invincible might, and they therefore appealed to Britain for assistance, under the Anglo-Dutch alliance. Burke's gloomiest prophecies were being fulfilled: republican boasts were being justified by grandiose achievements.

Pitt and his colleagues watched events take their sorry course. They were disgusted by the September massacres, concerned for the future of Louis XVI, and infuriated by the arrogance of the French minister of marine, who had offered help to the British republicans in abolishing the monarchy—'we will hurl thither fifty thousand caps of liberty!' Yet the withdrawal of the British ambassador from Paris was accompanied by the assurance that His Majesty's government had no intention of meddling in the internal affairs of France, and although Chauvelin lost his official status as French ambassador when Louis XVI was deposed, he was allowed to reside in London in a private capacity. Pitt did not want war, and he was doing everything possible to prevent it, but, like other British ministers in more recent times, he was to learn that goodwill was powerless to check naked aggression. He could not control the extremists in Paris, where virtue was inculcated by terror and failure punished by death, and he could not ignore Dutch pleas for help, or the traditional British solicitude for the independence of the Low Countries. At an earlier stage he had been satisfied by a French avowal that their troops would withdraw from the Austrian Netherlands on the cessation of hostilities, but now he was worried by their designs on Holland. Memories of 1787 stirred in his mind. When the French, advocating the extension of the republic one and indivisible to its 'natural' frontiers, annexed Savoy, Pitt detected the raw temptations of power in the conduct of the new rulers of France. But he remained cautious, determined to stay out of the conflict if it was possible to do so without losing prestige. In November 1792, before the publication of the Edict of Fraternity, he had explained his position to the Marquis of Stafford:

> . . . It seems absolutely impossible to hesitate as to supporting our ally in case of necessity, and the explicit declaration of our sentiments is the most likely way to prevent the case recurring. We have, therefore, thought it

best to send without delay instructions to Lord Auckland to present a memorial to the States. . . . I likewise enclose a copy of instructions to Sir Morton Eden in Berlin, and those to Vienna are very nearly to the same effect. These are necessarily in very general terms, as, in the ignorance of the designs of Austria and Prussia, and in the uncertainty as to what events each day may produce, it seems impossible to decide definitely at present the line which we ought to pursue, except as far as relates to Holland. Perhaps some opening may arise which may enable us to contribute to the termination of the war between the different powers of Europe, leaving France (which I believe is the best way) to arrange its own internal affairs as it can. The whole situation, however, becomes so delicate and critical, that I have thought it right to request the presence of all the members of the cabinet who can, without too much inconvenience, give their attendance. . . .

To the last moment Pitt strove to avoid war, but he underestimated the fanaticism of the Jacobins. Flushed with victory in the field, and elated by the carnage of foes at home, they proceeded to try the King. On 21 January 1793 Louis XVI, the bewildered victim of forces he had never understood, met his death on the scaffold, his final appeal to his people being drowned in the rattle of Santerre's drums. Danton urged a policy of boldness, throwing down the head of a King as the gage of battle, and on 1 February the republic declared war on Britain and Holland. Pitt's hopes were dashed. Britain faced a foe animated by a new ideal, and threatening not only the ordeal of arms but the destruction of society.

At home the situation was far from reassuring. In 1791 the Birmingham crowds had rioted for Church and King, burning Joseph Priestley's library, and driving him to seek asylum in the United States. But in 1792 the popular movements assumed a different character. Reports told of the 'disagreeable spirit amongst the common people' in Leicester, Nottingham, and Birmingham, whilst Dundas noted that all attempts to do mischief in Scotland centred in towns where manufactures were flourishing: Edinburgh, Glasgow, Paisley, Perth, Dundee, and Aberdeen. The dockers were on strike in Liverpool, and in Wigan the miners also came out. There were rumours of Jacobinical plots, fears of imminent revolution, and ugly bread riots. In the previous year Burke had solemnly warned the Commons of the secret manufacture of weapons for the use of the mob when the revolution came. He had thrown a dagger on to the floor of the House to drive his point home, but Sheridan had spoilt the gesture by asking 'Where's the fork?' The Members, not a little amused by Burke's violence, had laughed in glee. Now those who had thought Burke deranged in his obsession with the French Revolution outdid him in zeal. French spies were seen everywhere. *Emigrés*, priests and nobles alike, were suspected of being republican agents. No one cared to draw the parallel between the English and French Revolutions: disillusionment was widespread and bitter. Samuel Romilly, who had been unshaken as late as May 1792 in his opinion that the revolution was a 'most glorious' event, could not condone the September massacres:

> How could we ever be deceived in the character of the French nation as to think them capable of liberty! Wretches, who, after all their professions and boasts about liberty and patriotism, and courage, and dying, and after taking oath on oath, at the very moment when their country is invaded and the enemy is marching through unresisted, employ whole days in murdering women, and priests, and prisoners!

Robert Burns, who veered between careless statements of sympathy for the French and avowals of loyalty to the constitution (after all, he had his job as an exciseman to consider), deplored the annexation of Savoy and the invasion of Holland, while a radical like Thelwall contrasted the laudable principles of the revolution with the bestial practice of the revolutionaries. After 10 August 1792, Arthur Young lamented the transition from light to darkness, from liberty to slavery, whilst William Wordsworth, his youthful idealism shattered, saw the doom of freedom 'with anger vexed, with disappointment sore'. To a bluff Englishman like Cobbett 'the whole history of the French Revolution presents us with nothing but a regular progress in robbery and murder'.

To all who saw a terrible connection between revolutionary bloodshed in Paris and discontent at home, the radical societies offered foolish provocation. Respectable gentlemen feared the worst when the London Corresponding Society, with the shoemaker Hardy at its head, sent out the following message on 29 November 1792 to similar organisations throughout the country: 'Unless we are greatly deceived the time is approaching when the Object for which we struggle is likely to come within our reach.' This could easily be read in a revolutionary sense, and when the same society, in the person of John Frost, presented an address to the French Convention, congratulating it and asserting that revolutions would come 'easy' after the example given by the French, the link between Jacobin principles and popular agitation in England seemed proved beyond all shadow of doubt. In fact, the radicals looked back to Locke, rather than to Rousseau and Robespierre: they emphasised that government was a trust on behalf of the people, and demanded manhood suffrage, low taxation, and annual Parliaments. They were seeking political recognition, not social revolution or economic justice. The movement gained a great measure of support from the lower middle classes—craftsmen, small shop-keepers, teachers, and dissenting ministers, and many of these were later shocked by the irreligious policies of the French. They were, for the most part, very far from being Jacobins, but they had only themselves to blame when the government interpreted their enthusiasm for French styles of address as indicative of a more profound identity of motive and conviction.

The existence of societies whose function was the propagation of radical ideas created new problems for the government. The ardour inspired by the happy coincidence of the anniversary of the English Revolution with the outbreak of the French had given the cause of reform a new lease of life. The Society for Constitutional Information, originally founded in 1780, was revived: its principal activity was the distribution of progressive literature. More important was the London Corresponding Society, whose contribution of a penny a week gave it a wider appeal than the more exclusive Society for Constitutional Information, and the aristocratic Friends of the People—founded by Grey and Sheridan to campaign for the reform of Parliament. The Corresponding Society was in communication with other societies in the industrial towns, and the authorities were faced with a serious attempt to organise the forces of discontent, especially in the expanding towns of the north. Sheffield was particularly disquieting. Without a police force the situation was extremely unpleasant, and it was felt that the agitators had shown great judgment in selecting the city as the centre of their 'machinations'. Earl Fitzwilliam, with his estates in Yorkshire to think about, was troubled by the unrest in the West Riding. Nor was it surprising that the propertied classes took alarm when a Convention met at Edinburgh in December 1792, with representatives from over eighty societies in attendance. The conscious evocation of the French example was sinister: here was a movement

far different from the Yorkshire Association, and much more dangerous. Christopher Wyvill, who had played so distinguished a part in
that organisation's history, was convinced that the country was
'drawing near to a more serious crisis than ever before experienced'.
He had seen the diffusion of Paine's doctrines with horror, and these
were spreading 'not only at Sheffield and Manchester, but also in the
neighbourhood of Leeds and Wakefield . . . in Scotland and Ireland to
a very uncanny degree'. He confessed that, had he realised what was
afoot earlier, he 'certainly should have expressed . . . detestation of the
man . . . with greater force and vehemence'. As a clergyman, he found
Paine's jaunty free-thinking repugnant, and the social doctrines of
Part II of *The Rights of Man* made it more obnoxious than Part I.
Reform was now being urged, not by those who liked to talk in
suitably abstract terms of the 'people', but, embarrassingly enough, by
the people themselves.

But one figure remained true to his original advocacy of the essential
justice of the French Revolution. Fox obstinately refused to revise his
opinion that the revolution was primarily an attack on absolute
monarchy: not even the worst excesses of the Paris mob, or the cruel
dictatorship of the Committee of Public Safety, could alter the fundamental issue. In the struggle between France and the central powers he
took the former's part. Kellermann's victory at Valmy inspired him:
'No public event, not excepting Saratoga and Yorktown, ever happened that gave me so much delight. I would not allow myself to
believe it for some days for fear of disappointment.' The September
massacres—in sorry contrast—were 'the most heart-breaking event that
ever happened', yet he staunchly held to his original thesis. The confused state of France filled him with alarm: if the disorders terminated
in the re-establishment of 'ancient despotism' he had no doubt that this
would be 'a decisive blow to all liberty in Europe, at least for centuries'.
His love of liberty—generous, vague, passionate—was excited by the
spectacle of the French people struggling valiantly against foreign
invasion. He had always opposed any intervention in the domestic
affairs of France, and now it seemed that what he had feared had come
to pass: the suppression of the freedom which had been so hardly
earned, the grim restoration of feudal tyranny.

Yet, for all his enthusiasm for the French cause, he was not blind to
the dangers at home. Ironically, for a period in 1792, his outlook was

very similar to that of Pitt. Fox doubted the wisdom of pressing for
Parliamentary reform in circumstances of exceptional difficulty. He
disapproved of the Friends of the People, wryly commenting that its
founders seemed determined not to listen to any advice, and particularly not to pay any attention to his. However warmly he wished
for 'a moderate reform in the system of our representation', he did not
agree that 'the present was the proper season for the agitation of the
question'. He still looked forward to the time when reform would be
possible, but his motives were elusive and perplexing. On 16 March
1792 he told Fitzwilliam:

> I am more bound by former declarations and consistency, than by any
> strong opinion I entertain in its favour. I am far from being sanguine that
> any new scheme would produce better Parliaments than the present mode
> of election has furnished; but perhaps the House of Commons in the
> present reign has been so dragged through the dirt and bespattered, in the
> early times by the whigs, and in later by the King and Pitt and the Tories
> that one constructed on a new plan might be better from the mere
> circumstance of its novelty.

A curiously disillusioned motive for reform! Here he was writing as
an embittered party leader, but, though he disapproved of Grey's
motion calling for Parliamentary reform, he felt it his duty to support
it in the Commons. He was always liable to be moved by appeals to
his feelings, by the loyalty one old friend owed to another, and in his
political as well as his private life he often acted on impulse.

Such was the situation when the first moves were made to bring
over some of the whigs to the ministry. Burke regretted Pitt's failure
to be explicit about the measures necessary for the maintenance of
order, but he and Windham were convinced that Portland, Fitzwilliam,
and the aristocratic whigs should strengthen the ministry at a time of
crisis. They were certainly more voluble than Pitt, in demanding
repressive measures for dealing with the discontent in the northern
towns, but Burke's impetuosity put Portland and his friends in a
dilemma. In April, at a meeting at Burlington House, the conservative
wing of the party decided to oppose Grey's plan of reform. This
division was no new thing: the whig opposition, like Pitt's Cabinet,
had always disagreed over Parliamentary reform. But, in the peculiar
circumstances of 1792, such conduct was open to a more decisive interpretation. Was a negotiation with the minister intended? Certainly,

Pitt had an exaggerated idea of the divisions within the whig opposition, and when it became known that he had discussed the possibilities of negotiation with Burke and Windham, many of the whigs, already torn by the conflicting demands of friendship and political conviction, reacted indignantly to the suggestion that Pitt was playing upon their differences with their companions. Fox resented that he had not been approached first, and he suspected Burke of encompassing the total destruction of the whig party. He talked of attempts to 'pervert' Portland and Fitzwilliam, and vowed that he would only join a genuine coalition, on equal terms with the minister.

There were tentative proposals for Pitt and Fox to serve together as Secretaries of State, under a nominal head of the ministry. Such a plan attracted the Duke of Leeds, who conveniently saw himself presiding over just such an arrangement, but it was received with stony disdain by Pitt. He had no intention of humbling himself before old foes: why should he save them from the consequences of their own folly? Was it realistic to picture Fox and himself in happy partnership under an anonymous chief? His attitude was simple, precise, and unshaken: if any members of the opposition believed a national ministry was desirable, they were free to give their support, perhaps their services. But he would not give up his own position as First Lord of the Treasury: on that point there could be no bargaining. Portland, never a lucid thinker, floundered. He could not support Grey over reform, or Fox over the revolution. Yet he was bound to Fox by many intimate ties, and he had no wish to desert him. Ratting had no charms for the honest Duke. Unlike Burke, he could not resign himself to the loss of friends, and however much he was troubled by fears of disorder and social upheaval, he could not bring himself to go over to Pitt. So he and his friends clung to the hope that events, which had thrust them so callously into such anguish, would rescue them from their predicament. Perhaps Fox would realise his errors and moderate his point of view. Perhaps the situation in France might improve. But Fox's conduct was far from reassuring. He became more violent, not less so, and flung himself into the most uncompromising opposition. Suspicious, as ever, of the influence of the Crown, and sceptical of the motives underlying the cautious overtures which had been made to the more conservative members of the opposition, he ostentatiously adopted a position which emphasised his disagreement with his old colleagues. When he heard, at the beginning of December 1792 that the ministers were calling out the militia, he was enraged. Fitzwilliam was scandalised by his behaviour: 'I have seen Charles Fox . . . I by no means like him.' The weaknesses in his character, and the demands of a uniquely exacting situation, drove him into a course of action which was politically disastrous. While the Portland whigs were reluctant to oppose the ministry, Fox swore an oath, declaring 'there was no address at this moment Pitt could frame he would not propose an amendment to, and divide the House upon'. The ministers were little less than monsters in Fox's eyes. Frustrated ambition, the disappointment of high hopes and great expectations, perhaps the sheer habit of opposition, had driven Fox into a cul-de-sac from which there was no escape. His defence of English liberties was valuable during the long years of war and repression, but his motives were a mixture of the base as well as the noble. He had accepted too easily Anstruther's suggestion, that he had only to 'stand forward and load Pitt as the author of the present state of the country and run down his whole system of foreign politics', for the government to be compelled to resign.

The whig party was now finished. The rift with Burke was irreparable, and while Portland hesitated the desertion began in 1793. Malmesbury, who had gone over to the whigs in 1788, returned to the ministerial fold, and Loughborough, no longer prepared (as in 1783 and 1788) to sacrifice his legitimate ambitions to the demands of party, began the negotiations which finally brought him to the coveted Woolsack. Twenty-one members of the opposition followed the example of Burke and Windham and supported the government. Portland and Fitzwilliam did not go over until 1794, but the whig party, which Edmund Burke had devoted a lifetime to create, had ceased to exist. It had owed its inception to the tumultuous early years of George III's reign. Now a greater crisis broke its frail unity, and exposed the contradictions which had bedevilled it for so long. Pitt welcomed the allegiance of erstwhile opponents, but he neither wooed them nor feared them. When Addington asked him, after the final adherence of Portland and Fitzwilliam to the ministry, 'Are you not afraid that you might be outvoted in your own cabinet?' he answered, 'I am under no anxiety on that account. I place much dependence on my new colleagues; and I place still more dependence on myself.' The tribulations of the 1790s could not break this confidence, however rigorously they tested it. But Pitt could not overlook the inflexibility which the Portland whigs showed towards the republican régime in France, and their vociferous demands for stern measures to stamp out disaffection at home.

Radical agitation and demonstrations for cheap bread and an end to the war had their origins in the sufferings of the common people. Dismal harvests played a greater part than Jacobin spies in animating peremptory calls for reform. But ministers who were preoccupied with the French menace, and who had little knowledge and less experience of life in the industrial towns (how many of them had they even seen?), were ill-equipped to comprehend this blunt fact. Consequently, repression was the order of the day, a policy born of fear and of the horror engendered by the example of the fall of the French monarchy. To quail before disorder was to be overcome by it, and Pitt and his colleagues never forgot this during those years of fortitude, hardship, and disappointment.

Throughout the last, grey months of uneasy peace, the government had watched the growth of the radical societies with baffled concern. After the outbreak of the war the authorities went over to the offensive. Descriptions of the government as 'a corrupt and overbearing faction, which at present tramples on the rights and liberties of Englishmen' only heightened the prevalent cry for repression. The radicals showed an absurd lack of tact: John Frost explained his remark 'I am for equality', which was overheard in a public house, by the even more damaging admission, 'There ought to be no kings.' Talk like this, allied to the studied imitation of French precedents, only provoked savage revulsion amongst the upper classes, with the exception of eccentrics like Earl Stanhope, or overt sympathisers like Charles James Fox. The use of the word 'Citizen' might be no more than a harmless conceit, but it linked the leaders of the Convention in Britain with the less amicable members of the Convention in Paris, and when the radicals, who were principally interested in a political programme not unlike that of the Chartists, called Parliament 'a scoundrel sink of corruption' their revolutionary intentions seemed apparent. The people of England were reminded of their misfortunes:

> You are plunged into war by a wicked ministry and a compliant Parliament, who seem careless and unconcerned for your interest, the end and design of which is almost too horrid to relate, the destruction of a whole

people merely because they will be free. . . . Your treasure is wasting fast: the blood of your brethren is pouring out, and all this to form chains for a free people, and eventually to rivet them on yourselves.

The London Corresponding Society prepared to hold a Convention in 1794, and amongst the inflammatory propaganda which it sent out was the following chorus:

> Plant, plant the tree, fair Freedom's tree,
>   Midst dangers, wounds, and slaughter:
> Each patriot's breast its soil shall be,
>   And tyrants' blood its water.

Language of this sort could easily be cited as conclusive proof of the existence (as Pitt claimed) of

an enormous torrent of insurrection, which would sweep away all the barriers of government, law, and religion, and leave our country a naked waste for usurped authority to range in, uncontrolled and unresisted.

It was not surprising that several leading agitators were arrested and tried: had they limited themselves to pleading the case for reform on the lines adopted in the 1780s Pitt might not have stirred, but the mingling of Paine's theories and French practice, together with the pressure put upon him by aristocrats who feared the movement's social implications, compelled him to take action, and ultimately to condone conduct which not even the passage of one hundred and seventy years can make less repugnant.

In England, however, the trials were scrupulously fair. The Lord Chief Justice presided with admirable disinterestedness, and even Sir John Scott, who abhorred the defendants' principles, handled the prosecution in an honest and upright fashion. His thoroughness wearied the jury, one gentleman telling Adolphus, the historian, many years later, that even if the evidence had been much stronger 'I should have had great difficulty in convicting men of a crime when it took the Attorney-General nine hours to tell us what it was!' Hardy, Horne Tooke, and Thelwall were all charged with high treason, and all were acquitted. Erskine conducted the defence with great skill: during the trial of Horne Tooke in October 1794, Pitt himself appeared in the witness box, to testify to the part he had formerly played in the movement for Parliamentary reform. After a retirement of only eight minutes, the jury pronounced the defendant not guilty amidst scenes of rejoicing. Thelwall was a more difficult client. 'I'll be hanged if I don't plead my own cause!' he scribbled in a note to his counsel, only to receive the reply, 'You'll be hanged if you do!'; but the result was another acquittal. Frost was less fortunate: he was sentenced to six months' imprisonment for sedition, and struck off the role of attorneys, but in his case, too, Pitt's earlier career as a reformer was used to point the contrast between his former conduct and present opinions.

But in Scotland the course of justice had been far different. Braxfield struck out with a ferocious savagery which horrified public opinion. 'God help the nation that has such judges!' Fox cried in exasperation: he felt justifiable relief that he had succeeded in getting his Libel Bill through Parliament in 1792. Braxfield, who afterwards admitted that he did not know that sentences of transportation involved hard labour and penal servitude, welcomed the shameless packing of the juries for the Edinburgh trials—'Come awa', Maister Horner, come awa', and help us hang ane of the damned scoundrels.' He lectured the defendants, the juries, and the public on constitutional principles: 'As for the rabble, who have nothing but personal property, what hold has the nation of them?' he asked, and when Thomas Muir's bearing inspired respect amongst the public benches, he confessed, 'The indecent applause which was given Mr. Muir . . . convinces me that a spirit of discontent still lurks in the minds of the people.' Muir was despatched to Australia for fourteen years, and in September 1793 Thomas Palmer, a distinguished, if rash and imprudent, Unitarian minister, and a former Fellow of Queens' College, Cambridge, was sentenced to seven years' transportation.

Grey and Sheridan attacked the severity of the sentences, and no doubt they were acutely aware of the dangers of Braxfield's definition of sedition:

> endeavouring to create a disaffection in the country, which nobody can tell where it will end. It will very naturally end in rebellion; and if it has that tendency, though not in the mind of the parties at the time, yet, if they have been guilty of poisoning the minds of the lieges, I apprehend that it will constitute the crime of sedition to all intents and purposes.

Pitt, in one of the most discreditable episodes of his career, upheld the Scottish judiciary. Although the responsibility for Scottish affairs was shouldered by Dundas, the indifference of Pitt, a trained lawyer, to the perversion of justice, was a saddening sight. Fox pleaded for compassion in noble language; Grey maintained that Muir had been transported for doing what Pitt himself had done twelve years before; but the sentences stood. The ministers loyally supported the officers of the law, and Loughborough, so lately the colleague of those who denounced Braxfield's inhumanity, dismissed pleas for mercy with contempt—'to save the country from revolution the authority of all tribunals, high and low, must be upheld'. The radical agitators had been foolish and provocative, but scarcely criminal: they suffered for the sins of the republicans in Paris.

The capitulation of thinking people to the fears and prejudices of the hour was distressing, but understandable. As well as fighting a war against a ruthless foe, the country was undergoing a social revolution, and a sequence of bleak summers and bad harvests had created much hardship. Even Pitt, usually so icily superior to common feelings and popular opinion, was not immune from the 'anti-Jacobin' scare, though he panicked less than many of his associates. If the exigencies of national defence can be cited in palliation of the excesses of the French revolutionaries, the same extenuation can be made, with as much justification, for the British government, and, by Parisian standards, Pitt's 'reign of terror' was mild indeed, despite Dundas's spies. Some historians have claimed that the policy of repression strengthened, not weakened, the radical movement; others that it was haphazardly enforced by easy-going magistrates, that Portland, the Home Secretary, however much he called for measures to protect property, lacked the energy to apply the law with an intensity equal to that with which the French Jacobins exterminated all opposition in the name of national unity. Auckland believed that nine-tenths of the country were loyal, and the nation's acquiescence to the anti-Jacobin legislation—the Aliens Act of 1792, the Seditious Meetings Act, the Treasonable Correspondence Act, the suspension of Habeas Corpus, the anti-Combination Laws of 1799—implies general agreement. To be anti-French was to be pro-Pitt, and most of the common people, however grim their struggle against the age-old enemies of poverty, hunger, disease, and death, had no wish to follow the French example. That the roots of discontent lay deeper than any regard for the latest fashions in Paris is shown by the way in which agitation and popular demonstrations coincided with bad harvests, high prices, and food shortages.

In 1795, when the Corresponding Society met at St. George's fields, the delegates condemned the high price of food, as well as demanding annual Parliaments and universal manhood suffrage. They wanted a 'speedy and lasting peace', and in order to get it they called for 'the acknowledgement of the brave French Republic'. But they wanted peace because they wanted bread, not because they admired the Jacobin constitution. At Birmingham the crowds cried for a large loaf, and there were similar bread riots in Nottingham, Coventry, and Sussex. The London mob shouted 'No war! No famine! No Pitt!' breaking the minister's windows in Downing Street to slake their rage. Pitt was not put out, assuring his mother that all was well: though his windows had been 'visited . . . with a single pebble' the crowd 'was really so young and so little versed in its business that it hardly merited the notice of a newspaper' (18 July 1795). In October the King was given a rowdy reception on his way to open Parliament, and on his arrival the imperturbable monarch announced, 'My Lords, I have been shot at.' The whigs scoffed at the 'Pop-gun Plot', alleging that the affair had been stage-managed by the government to justify their repressive policy. But, although the King and Queen were greeted with a magnificent ovation on the following evening when they attended the theatre at Covent Garden, the ministers saw the incident as fraught with danger, as an undeniable indication that it was impossible to err on the side of caution.

The demand for peace—for an end to the seemingly endless hostilities —was great, however much Burke thundered against any negotiation with the regicide republic, describing a 'change in the national spirit' as 'the most terrible of all revolutions'. Pitt tried to come to terms with the Directory, whose corruption held out hopes of moderation, but Grenville's pessimism seemed justified when informal overtures ended in frustration in March 1796. The French refused to give up any of their conquests, whilst insisting that the British returned their acquisitions in the West Indies. Pitt rightly claimed that such an attitude 'if persevered in . . . must be an eternal obstacle to the conclusion of any peace'. In October another effort was made. Malmesbury opened discussions with the French Foreign Minister, Delacroix, but the refusal of the Directory to restore Belgium to the Austrians caused the negotiations to founder, and in December, Malmesbury was ordered to leave Paris within forty-eight hours—a humiliating conclusion to the conversations. Pitt felt 'deep and poignant regret' at this rebuff, but it only stiffened his resolve: 'we are not yet arrived at so deplorable a state of wretchedness and abasement as to be compelled to make any insecure and dishonourable compromise'.

> In fact [he told the Commons on 30 December 1796], the question is not, how much you will give for peace, but how much disgrace you will suffer at the outset, how much degradation you will submit to as a preliminary. In these circumstances, then, are we to persevere in the war with a spirit and energy worthy of the British name and of the British character; or are we, by sending couriers to Paris, to prostrate ourselves at the feet of a stubborn and supercilious Government, to do what they require, and to submit to whatever they may impose?

Yet, although he had little doubt of the nation's response, the war had gone badly. In February 1793 Pitt, like most of his contemporaries, had anticipated a speedy end to the conflict. When the King took the salute as the Guards marched off to Greenwich on the first stage of their journey to Holland, no one in the huge crowd thought that the campaign would be anything other than short, sharp, and victorious. Hopes were high after Dumouriez's defeat at Neerwinden, and his subsequent desertion to the allies, but the young Duke of York's little expeditionary force was soon involved in Coburg's snail-like advance, and when the Austrian commander found himself before Condé and Valenciennes he dutifully halted in the approved eighteenth-century style in order to reduce both fortresses. Throughout the summer Pitt fretted impatiently for good news from Flanders. When the towns surrendered in July their garrisons were allowed to march home: the commanders of the allied armies expected their adversaries to behave like gentlemen, and to abide by the rules of war. The French, liberated by revolutionary fervour from subservience to outmoded standards of conduct, diverted these troops to the task of subduing the peasants of La Vendée, who had risen in royalist enthusiasm and Catholic zeal against the republic. As the first year of the war ended, the great opportunity for winning it slipped away from the over-cautious allies. The great advance—infelicitously described by Lord Hawkesbury as 'the march on Paris'—petered out in stalemate, and the campaign in the Low Countries saw the British army stranded at Ostend. The insurrection at Toulon, put down for the republic by a young artillery officer called Bonaparte, embroiled the British in the struggle between the various French factions, and, however eloquently Burke and his friends pleaded the Bourbon cause, Pitt was out of his depth. The allies tempted Providence by wasting their chances: the dilatory defenders of the Old Order learned in the stern school of experience that republican France could not be given the smallest breathing space.

The demand for indemnities, for a piece of territory here or a frontier town there, together with the threat of a Bourbon restoration, had made the cause of the republic that of France. Patriotism was identified with the tricolour, not the lilies, and, whilst Carnot and Danton roused the nation against the enemy abroad, the guillotine looked after the traitor at home. Marie Antoinette followed her husband to the scaffold, bearing the insults of her trial and the jeers of the mob with dignity and courage. But other heads rolled: in Vergniaud's poignant and un-forgettable phrase, the revolution, like Saturn, was devouring its own children. The Girondins, who had gone to war with a light heart, paid for their folly with their lives, and, while Madame Roland invoked the spirit of Liberty by lamenting the crimes committed in its name, other Girondins met death less nobly. Hunted down like wild beasts, several took their own lives: some bungled even their attempts at suicide. The struggle for power continued within the Jacobin Club, and Robespierre, the purest disciple of Jean-Jacques Rousseau, looked askance at the lecherous atheism of Hébert, at the sight of the Goddess of Reason personified by a whore. He was also disturbed by Danton's growing disposition to be merciful, and by playing off Hébert, the author of obscenities, against Danton, the apologist for leniency, he destroyed both. Danton, the patriot, died as he had lived. The thought of his young wife unnerved him in the tumbril, but, ascending the scaffold amidst pools of blood, and silhouetted against the setting sun, he was defiant—'Come, Danton, no weakness!'—and ordered the executioner, 'Show my head to the people—it is worth it!' With Robespierre in control, the terror intensified. The representatives on mission subjugated the provinces and inspired the armies. The reign of virtue replaced licence, and the Feast of the Supreme Being succeeded the worship of Reason. Rousseau's civil religion had arrived.

But, mystifying and appalling as the changes were in the govern-ment of France, they made little difference to the success of her armies. Victory thrived on terror. The French triumph at Fleurus necessitated the withdrawal of the British expeditionary force from Flanders, and gave the Duke of York the opportunity to prove that he was as capable an administrator as he had been inept as a commander in the field. Howe's victory of the 'Glorious First of June' thrilled British hearts with the knowledge that the navy could still beat any French fleet that dared to challenge it, but the admiral had failed to accomplish his strategic objective—the destruction of the convoy bringing much needed grain to a half-starving France. Villaret-Joyeuse lost a battle, but he saved France. In 1795 the Prussians, more adept at taking British subsidies than in waging campaigns against the Republic, and greedily contemplating the acquisition of another slice of Poland, left the coalition. In June of the same year the Quiberon expedition sailed—an attempt to assist the French royalists who were giving their lives with a courage worthy of Princes nobler than the shallow Artois, who neither shared their tribulations, nor appreciated their sacrifices. Incompetent and divided command, poor organisation, and rampant jealousies resulted in ignominious withdrawal in December, and the revolt in Brittany was ruthlessly crushed. In July 1795 Spain, too, made peace with France, and in the following year, inspired by Godoy's concept of duplicity as the surest guide in diplomacy, she joined her late foe as an ally. The fall of Robespierre, and the substitution of the dissolute régime of the Directory for the austere reign of virtue, had not changed the fortunes of war. Terror was no longer necessary, for its purpose—the defeat of the invader—had been achieved. Now France was on the offensive on every front. Young General Bonaparte, whose whiff of grapeshot had made him into the saviour of society, was given command of the Army of Italy on the initiative of one of his wife's old lovers. In his brilliant Italian campaign he smashed the Austrians in a series of victories which left the ponderous Imperial army breathless and demoralised. In the autumn of 1797 the Emperor accepted the terms of Campo Formio. Britain stood alone.

Pitt was no gifted strategist and his attitude to the war was a narrowly practical one. George III thought that everyone concerned for the preservation of civilisation ought to stand forth against the French, 'that most savage as well as unprincipled nation', and Burke, deriding a war for the Scheldt as a war for a chamber-pot, called for a European crusade. But Pitt did not share such indignation. The violation of solemn international pledges worried him more than generalised talk about crusades to cleanse the world. He knew, of course, that the war had been precipitated by French aggression, and that this aggression was, in part, the consequence of their principles. In February 1793 he had spoken of the need for France to renounce aggrandizement and to confine herself within her own frontiers if she wanted to maintain friendly relations with Britain. On the same day that the French Convention had declared war on Great Britain, he had told the Commons that although the country desired peace, it would have to be

> such as may be real and solid, and consistent with the interests and dignity of Britain and the general security of Europe. War, whenever it comes, will be preferable to peace without honour, without security, and which is incompatible either with the external peace or the internal happiness of this country.

On 12 February he had defended the government's record with reference to France:

> We have, in every instance, observed the strictest neutrality with respect to the French: we have pushed, to its utmost extent, the system of temperance and moderation; we have held out the means of accommodation; we have waited till the last moment for satisfactory explanation. . . . They have now, at last, come to actual aggression, by seizing our vessels in their very ports, without any provocation given on our part. Without any preparations having been adopted but those of necessary precaution, they have declared, and are now waging, war. Such is the conduct which they have pursued; such is the situation in which we stand. It now remains to be seen whether under Providence, the efforts of a free, brave, loyal, and happy people, aided by their allies, will not be successful in checking the progress of a system, the principles of which, if not opposed, threaten the most fatal consequences to the tranquillity of this country, the security of its allies, the good order of every European Government, and the happiness of the whole human race!

He was aware of the danger from French principles, but he was more distressed by the dangers from French cannon. Yet he could not, at this stage, devise any overall strategy for the war. The 'blue-water' concept, which had been so successful in his father's day, was pursued with determination, but its relevance to the needs of the situation was doubtful. The republican government was not so worried by the loss of remote sugar islands and distant trading posts as the Bourbons had been: the Jacobins were too busy with problems nearer home. And, in the tropical climate of the West Indies, British troops died in thousands. Pitt was also over-optimistic about the strains imposed on French economy. His sympathy for economic theory, and his sanguine temperament, deceived him. Like others, he knew that the American War had brought the French monarchy to bankruptcy and disaster. The present conflict must surely do the same for the republic, and the catastrophic inflation which followed the issue of *assignats* sustained him in his belief. He forgot that the new régime defied the laws of finance, just as it ignored the conventions of war. He relied too much on the good faith of his allies, only to discover, with pained surprise, that all too often they accepted his payments without fulfilling their obligations. With the failure of Malmesbury's negotiation, and the retention by the French of their conquests—conveniently disguised under the fiction that they were 'independent' republics, an irony peculiarly bitter coming from a régime purporting to deny the facile frauds of traditional diplomacy—Pitt, deserted by his allies and sorely tried by troubles at home, braced himself for the next test.

In February 1797 a gloomy winter was brightened by Sir John Jervis's victory over the Spanish fleet at Cape St. Vincent, where Commodore Nelson thrust his two-decker H.M.S. *Captain* into the gap into the enemy's line of battle. Yet, within two months, even this was blighted by an event so astounding as to baffle belief: the fleet mutinied. At Spithead, Bridport's Channel squadron refused to sail. The sailors had many grievances: miserably low pay, foul food, harsh discipline, the memory of the press-gang. They asked for better wages, edible provisions, protection against exploitation, medical attention, and leave. Nor did they jeopardise their case by outrageous behaviour. If the enemy put to sea, they would sail to meet him, but they refused to act until their grievances had been remedied. The government gave way: they had little choice. The country was in peril, once the navy could not be relied upon. Howe, the sailors' beloved 'Black Dick', sailed round the ships with the King's pardon in his hand. The men instinctively distrusted the politicians, but they felt that the stubborn, brave old King was as good as his word.

Whilst the sailors of the Channel fleet were principally concerned to alleviate the brutal conditions under which they lived, the outbreak at the Nore was much more sinister. Richard Parker, who had joined the navy to escape a debtors' prison, introduced the element of the professional agitator, which had been wholly lacking in the strangely respectful, and ostentatiously loyal, mutiny at Spithead. He sought to use the legitimate grievances of the men to break down the customary structure of command: he was an egalitarian, demanding that officers should be dismissed at the behest of their men, and with the vanity of a revolutionary he refused to treat with anyone below the rank of Lords of the Admiralty. He acquired a taste for pomp and ceremony and a partiality for self-exaltation. But his hour of glory was brief. At first the mutiny had been popular throughout the fleet, but when the government confined the sailors to their ships and cut off the food supplies, grumbles against the new order became as common as hatred of the old. The mutineers tarred and feathered several officers, and threatened to blockade the Thames, but public opinion was now firmly on the side of the authorities, and the men began to doubt the wisdom and suspect the motives of their new masters. When it became known that Parker had withheld the offer of a royal pardon from the rank and file his spell was broken. The sailors realised the specious pretentiousness of his claims. One by one the ships returned to their allegiance. Parker and twenty-eight other ringleaders were hanged. Meanwhile robust Admiral Duncan, his command reduced to his flagship and a solitary frigate, deceived the Dutch by signalling to imaginary men-of-war over the horizon: it was vital that the enemy should not learn of the breach in England's wooden walls. In October the Dutch put to sea, but De Winter had lost his opportunity. Discipline was now restored in the British fleet and the sailors were burning to wipe out their disgrace by coming to grips with the foe. The shame of the Nore was expunged by the victory of Camperdown, and the Dutch Admiral, losing a game of whist in his captor's cabin, remarked that it was hard to be beaten twice in one day by the same opponent. Miraculously Britain had come through.

The strain on Pitt had been immense. Not only had he to face defeat and the defection of allies—both Spain and Holland were in arms against Great Britain—but prices soared and food was scarce. He could not ignore the cry for peace and bread, however much he might despise the breaking of his windows by the mob. In the summer of 1797 another attempt was made to come to some agreement with the Directory. Malmesbury was sent to Lille with generous terms. Since Austria had signed the preliminaries of Leoben in April, the British government no longer felt bound to insist on the restoration of Belgium to the Emperor. France was to keep all her continental conquests, while Britain offered to return all her prizes except the Cape of Good Hope and Trinidad. But the *coup d'état* of Fructidor meant the triumph of the war party in France, and Malmesbury was ignominiously expelled from the republic a second time. The ambitions of the French verged on megalomania: they coveted Canada, Newfoundland, the Channel Islands, and India, as well as demanding Gibraltar on behalf of their satellite, Spain. The collapse of negotiations was a bitter blow to Pitt, but he did not flinch. As he told the Commons on 10 November:

> This is not the moment to dwell only on our disappointment, to suppress our indignation, or to let our courage, our constancy, and our determination be buried in the expression of unmanly fear, or unavailing regret.

He had hoped that the moderate, pacific, party would gain control in France, thus 'opening the way to the happiest alterations in the general system of that country'; but the British representative had encountered duplicity, arrogance, and violence, and without good faith there could be no lasting peace. He disclaimed any animosity towards the people of France, but censured their government's outrageous demands. He appealed for new exertions:

> there may be danger; but on the one side there is danger accompanied with honour, on the other side there is danger with indelible shame and disgrace. Upon such an alternative Englishmen will not hesitate.

He put his trust in the national character,

> by which we have preserved our existence and fame as a nation, which I trust we shall be determined never to abandon under any extremity, but shall join hand and heart in the solemn pledge that is proposed to us, and declare to His Majesty, that we know great exertions are wanting, that we stand prepared to make them, and at all events determined to stand or fall by the laws, liberties, and religion of our country.

The reorganisation of the national finances could not meet the increased expenditure caused by the war. In February 1797 a run on the banks forced the government to suspend cash payments, and the Bank of England was permitted to issue paper currency—an expedient which inspired the jingle:

> *Of Augustus and Rome*
> *The poets still warble,*
> *How he found it of brick,*
> *And left it of marble.*

So of Pitt and of England
Men may say without vapour,
That he found it of gold,
And left it of paper!

Public confidence was not enhanced by the melancholy precedent of the *assignats* in France. Pitt had to find some means of increasing the government's income: a deficit of £19,000,000 had to be met. In 1798 he finally imposed the most revolutionary and unpopular of all fiscal burdens—the income tax. All who earned more than £60 a year were taxed. A sliding scale fixed the contributions up to £200: all whose annual income exceeded this sum paid what seemed to contemporaries the exorbitant assessment of 2s. in the pound. Nor was this the limit of official insolence. Existing taxes were increased, in some cases trebled, even quadrupled. Fox prophesied universal catastrophe, and the well-to-do showed a touching anxiety for the disastrous consequences of these measures on the labouring classes. Fanny Burney parted with four windows to reduce her liability. But, though Pitt's budget earned him the hisses of the mob, he had not misjudged the temper of the nation. However much they bemoaned the new taxes, men gave generously to the voluntary subscription which accompanied them. In their hearts they knew that further sacrifices were necessary. The King gave £20,000; Pitt £2000; the Duke of Bedford £100,000. Ordinary folk gave what they could: one ship's crew gave ten shillings each. Altogether two and a half million pounds were raised. The British would go down fighting—or drive the rascally French into the sea.

Pitt's devotion to duty impressed all who knew him. No one better exemplified 'the virtues of adversity endured and adversity resisted, of adversity encountered and adversity surmounted'. He drove himself hard, poring for long hours over huge War Office maps in Downing Street. While leaving Dundas (the Secretary for War) and Grenville (the Foreign Secretary) in charge of their departments, he actively supervised all the other Cabinet ministers. He did not allow official correspondence to be read for him. He did not trust subordinates to sort out material on his behalf. He liked to see for himself. Like another great prime minister when Britain was in peril he enjoyed the blessing of sound sleep. During the naval mutinies, Lord Spencer, a highly efficient First Lord of the Admiralty, consulted Pitt at Downing Street.

He had already retired, but, sitting up in bed, he gave Spencer his instructions. No sooner had the First Lord stepped into the street when he remembered another point on which he wanted Pitt's opinion. When he returned to the minister's bedroom he found him fast asleep. Unless the House was sitting Pitt dined most days at five, but, if he was thrown out of this routine, he became ill for a day or two. Eventually the tension of the war years undermined his health, but he bore it all in aloof silence. He was contemptuous of pleas for place, and scornful of advice he thought absurd, but he valued the opinions of those whose knowledge and integrity he could respect. Whenever a delegation from the London merchants told him of their problems he listened attentively. Nor was he indifferent to the sufferings of the poor. On one occasion, when staying in Essex with his private secretary, Joseph Smith, he commented on the affluence of the working classes. On the next day he was appalled when his host showed him the squalor and poverty of the neighbouring town of Halstead. Pitt had no idea that such degrading conditions existed. In November 1796 he laid his Poor Relief Bill before the Commons, endeavouring to forestall revolution by timely reform. It was a strange document, mingling the supplementation of wages out of the rates (the notorious expedient so unhappily resorted to by the well-meaning magistrates at Speenhamland) with crude provisions for old-age pensions and schools of industry. Parishes were to train children in a craft, and to afford employment to the destitute. The Bill was harshly criticised. The experts pronounced it economically unsound, and Jeremy Bentham subjected it to his corroding sarcasm. Pitt was compelled to withdraw the measure for revision, and the financial crisis of 1797 ensured that such a wasteful and extravagant piece of legislation was not reintroduced. Its importance, as a primitive experiment in social security, can be exaggerated, but it indicated Pitt's concern for the problems of destitution and unemployment.

During the winter of 1796–1797 Pitt spent much time at Eden Farm, the home of the Auckland family, which was near his own residence at Holwood. He was often in the company of Eleanor Eden, Lord Auckland's eldest daughter, and a pretty and sprightly girl. Rumours hinted at marriage, but, even in December 1796, Auckland was cautious, admitting no more than that his daughter was 'possessed of sense far superior to the ordinary proportion of the world; they see

20 THE NUPTIAL BOWER

'To the Nuptial Bower he led her Blushing like the Morn'; with the Evil One peeping at the charms of Eden

From a caricature by James Gillray, 1797

21   WILLIAM PITT
Detail from the bust by Joseph Nollekens

much of each other, they converse together, and I believe they have sentiments of mutual esteem'. At the beginning of the new year the newspapers referred to the forthcoming match. Cartoons depicted the happy pair as Adam and Eve in the Garden of Eden, with Fox as the evil Serpent. Pitt was attracted to Miss Eden—the only instance of a romantic attachment in his life—but, in circumstances which remain mysterious, he decided that marriage was impossible. In one letter to Auckland he described the obstacles as 'decisive and insurmountable', and referred to any future husband as 'destined to more than his share of human happiness'. In another, he expressed his sorrow for any pain he had caused, adding: 'Believe me, I have not lightly or easily sacrificed my best hopes and earnest wishes to my conviction and judgment.' Despite the Wardenship of the Cinque Ports, which the King had conferred upon him after the death of Lord North, Pitt's private affairs were in hopeless confusion, and the situation was made all the more difficult by the knowledge that Auckland himself was not a wealthy man. Was it fair to ask a young woman, eighteen years his junior, to marry him in such circumstances? Throughout the brief, transient courtship he had behaved in an upright fashion, yet his conduct has been interpreted as just another proof of his heartlessness, of the superficiality of his feelings, and of that lack of virility, upon which his contemporaries descanted with unrestrained coarseness. But perhaps it demonstrates his honesty: if he could not make an honourable marriage he would make none at all. And he was the loser by his decision. Miss Eden made another match: Pitt lived out his bachelor existence at Downing Street and Walmer Castle, with his eccentric niece, Lady Hester Stanhope, as his housekeeper. Possibly he was too set in his ways to face the upheaval of matrimony, but, in an age embarrassed by the revelations of Freudian science and explanations derived from the unconscious mind, attempts at amateur psychiatry are ill-advised: it is dangerous to psychoanalyse the dead.

In the year of lonely defiance and perilous isolation, Pitt's health showed a marked deterioration. He suffered from recurrent headaches, which often lasted several days, as well as from stomach trouble and gout. The regularity of his hours was disturbed. He no longer breakfasted punctually at nine. He seldom rose before eleven, when he took a short ride, and, according to Addington, he remained addicted to staying in bed in the morning for the rest of his life. The doctors dispensed their prescriptions, and recommended the eighteenth-century cure for every mysterious or persistent ailment—a change of air. Certainly he benefited from week-ends at Walmer Castle, but, although there was some improvement during the autumn of 1797, he was not fully restored to health until the summer of 1798. In July of that year he confessed that he was growing stronger every day, but Auckland, glad as he was to see a definite recovery, was convinced that Pitt had been badly shaken. His spirits were good, but his diet, exercise, and hours all needed care and attention. Yet his mind remained as active as ever. He consoled himself for national reverses and personal disappointments by translating Horace:

> How bless'd, how glorious they who bravely fall,
> Their lives devoted, at their country's call!
> Death too pursues the coward as he flies;
> The dart o'ertakes him, and disgrac'd he dies.
> No mean repulse intrepid Virtue knows;
> Spotless and pure her native splendour glows;
> No gaudy ensigns her's, of borrow'd pow'r,
> No fame, dependent on the varying hour;
> Bowed to no yoke, her honours are her own,
> Nor court the breath of popular renown.
> On wing sublime resistless Virtue soars;
> And, spurning human haunts and earthly shores,
> To those whom godlike deeds forbid to die,
> Unbars the gates of Immortality.

To Pitt, wracked by illness, thwarted in love, and stricken yet again by family bereavement (his brother-in-law, Edward Eliot, died in September 1797, aged thirty-nine), the lines spoke with a personal voice.

In May 1798 he fought his famous duel with Tierney, in consequence of his refusal to withdraw the statement that the latter's opposition to the Navy Bill proceeded from 'a desire to obstruct the defence of the country'. His habitual self-control had deserted him in debate, and the pair, equally obstinate in vindicating their honour, exchanged shots on Wimbledon Common, fortunately with no ill-effects, Pitt discharging his second pistol in the air. Wilberforce was horrified by the incident, and gave notice of a motion in the Commons condemning duelling, but his good intentions only earned him a haughty rebuke. Pitt made it plain that such a motion would question the propriety of his own conduct, and Wilberforce, realising his sensitivity, allowed the matter to drop. It was left to George III to express popular feeling, when, with typical common sense, he reminded Pitt: 'Public characters have no right to weigh alone what they owe to themselves; they must consider also what is due to their country.' What was it that Burke had said? That men who wished to act greatly must suffer greatly? And now Burke, the most inflexible opponent of the French Revolution, and its greatest critic, was dead. Broken-hearted by the death of his son, dejected by the catastrophe which had overwhelmed all that he loved, he had died in July 1797, spurning any death-bed reconciliation with Fox and exhorting his countrymen to resist to the end: to die, if necessary, with swords in their hands. Two years before he had urged Pitt not to distrust his own faculties, his cause, or his country:

> Everything is arduous about you. But you are called to that situation, and you have abilities for it. . . . Our people have more in them than they exactly know of themselves. . . . There is one thing I pray for in your favour (for in you is our last human hope)—that you may not fall into the one great error from whence there is no return. I trust in the mercy of God to you, and to us all, that you may never be led to think that this war is, in its principles or in anything that belongs to it, the least resembling any other war; or that what is called a peace with the robbery of France can by any plan of policy be rendered reconcilable with the inward repose, or with the external strength, power, or influence of this kingdom. This, to me, is as clear as the light under the meridian sun; and this conviction, for these five years past and in the midst of other deep and piercing griefs, has cost me many an anxious hour at midday and at midnight. . . .

But Pitt's attitude to the conflict with France was far different. He was prepared to negotiate with the republican régime, however much he preferred a constitutional monarchy as the solution for France's woes. He was less unbending than his cousin, Grenville, on one occasion confessing: 'I feel it my duty, as an English minister and a Christian, to use every effort to stop so bloody and wasting a war.' Resolute in the face of misfortune, he had nevertheless no wish to perpetuate the struggle, if it should prove possible to terminate it. He was willing to bargain with the new order. He had never committed himself to the extreme ideological position adopted by Burke, and expounded by him with such force and eloquence. Pitt was no ideologue. Yet, while his moderation was denounced from the right, it also brought him into collision with the left. Burke condemned the government for treating with the Directors: Fox criticised the ministers for not being sufficiently enthusiastic, for failing to negotiate earlier. Until an exhausting series of defeats drove him to secede from the Commons—partly in disgust, partly because he was increasingly fond of the domestic bliss he knew at St. Anne's Hill—Fox attacked the ministry in a succession of brilliant speeches. With the verbal dexterity acquired in a lifetime of controversy, he exposed the inconsistencies of negotiating with a régime which had been stigmatised as untouchable, and decried the arrogant folly of passing judgment on the way the French ran their own affairs. Pitt and Grenville sought some security that any agreements made between Britain and the French Republic would be honoured by successive French governments. Fox claimed that, though France was groaning under a tyranny, the tyrants were capable of maintaining international relations with other powers:

> Did not the Brissotine party maintain the treaties of their predecessors? Did not the execrable tyrant Robespierre himself observe with equal fidelity the treaties made by Brissot? . . . It had been observed with truth that no one period in the French Revolution had been marked by a more sacred regard to the neutrality of foreign powers than the reign of that execrable tyrant Robespierre; and it would not be denied but that treaties had been made with tyrants as execrable; and considering what sort of treaties ministers had made, with whom they had made them, and what acts of base and abandoned tyranny they had not discountenanced, it was not worthy of the manly character of the British nation to abet them in their resistance to a treaty with France. [Debate of 9 December 1795.]

There was a deep irony in the fact that Fox, who had a more profound understanding of the appeal of the ideals of the French Revolution than Pitt, nevertheless thought of the war in traditional terms, and that he failed to see that the revolution had overturned all the old concepts of diplomacy and negotiation as surely as it had destroyed the French monarchy. Fox saw the parallel between the régime of terror and traditional autocracies. He did not perceive the more decisive differences of character, which made it difficult for the ministers to negotiate with the Directory. Many Englishmen regarded his sympathy with the successive stages of the revolution as little less than treason, and when Fox followed the Duke of Norfolk in 1797 in toasting the sovereignty of the people, George III struck his name off the Privy Council.

Pitt denied that he was seeking to restore the monarchy in France. 'Whatever', he said in the Commons debate of 7 June 1799,

> I may in the abstract think of the kind of government called a republic, whatever may be its fitness to the nation where it prevails, there may be times when it would not be dangerous to exist in its vicinity. But while the spirit of France remains what at present it is, its government despotic, vindictive, unjust, with a temper untamed, a character unchanged, if its power to do wrong at all remains, there does not exist any security for this country or for Europe. In my view of security, every object of ambition and aggrandisement is abandoned. Our simple object is security, just security, with a little admixture of indemnification. These are the legitimate objects of war at all times. . . . We shall not be satisfied with a false security. . . .

The war was not being waged against abstract sentiments:

> We are not in arms against the opinions of the closet, nor the speculations of the school. We are at war with armed opinions; we are at war with those opinions which the sword of audacious, unprincipled, and impious innovation seeks to propagate amidst the ruins of empires, the demolition of the altars of all religion, the destruction of every venerable and good and liberal institution, under whatever form of polity it has been raised. . . .

As long as the principles of the French Revolution had been the subject of intellectual debate,

> it was pleasing to regard them with respect; for, while the simplicity of the man of genius is preserved untouched, if we will not pay homage to his eccentricity, there is, at least, much in it to be admired. Whilst these principles were confined in that way and had not yet bounded over the common sense and reason of mankind, we saw nothing in them to alarm, nothing to terrify. But their appearance in arms changed their character. . . .

While France threatened the security of Europe war was inevitable:

> but if I should see any chance of the return of a government that did not threaten the existence of other governments, far be it from me to breathe hostility to it.

The difficulty (and Fox never tired of pointing this out) lay in assessing the permanence or stability of any new government in France; but, at the same time, the ideological character of the revolution, allied to the military prowess of the republican armies, created a situation of unique complexity. Again and again Pitt emphasised that security was the object of the war. In February 1800 he replied to Tierney's gibe that not one 'plain, satisfactory reason' could be given for the continuation of the war:

> He defies me to state in one sentence what is the object of the war. I know not whether I can do it in one sentence; but in one word I can tell him that it is *security*: security against a danger . . . which in degree and extent was never equalled. . . .

He was not resorting to 'special pleading': the conduct of the war was no light matter. Innumerable factors had to be borne in mind:

> The restoration of the French monarchy . . . would afford the strongest and best security to this country and to Europe. *But* this object may not be attainable; and *if* it be not attainable, we must be satisfied with the best security which we can find independent of it. Peace is most desirable to this country; *but* negotiation may be attended with greater evils than could be counterbalanced by any benefits which would result from it. And *if* this be found to be the case; *if* it afford no prospect of security; *if* it threaten all the evils which we have been struggling to avert; *if* the prosecution of the war afford the prospect of attaining complete security; and *if* it may be prosecuted with increasing commerce, with increasing means, and with increasing prosperity . . . then I say that it is prudent . . . not to negotiate at the present moment. These are my *buts* and *ifs*. This is my plea, and on no other do I wish to be tried by God and my country.

Those who thought that the war could be ended by means other than vigorous military operations were entitled to their opinion—'God forbid I should question the freedom of thought or the liberty of speech!'—but Pitt warned the House of the dangers of language 'contrary to all honest principle, and repugnant to every sentiment of public duty'.

However brilliant Fox's denunciations of the ministry's fluctuating attitude to the French Republic, however scintillating his appeals for a negotiated peace, the experience of dealing with a régime committed to the doctrine of permanent revolution makes possible a fuller appreciation of the tragic dilemma into which Pitt was thrust by events. Negotiation becomes a delusion when both parties interpret the same words, and specific undertakings, differently, and the exchange of views soon degenerates into a polite fiction cloaking the lack of real communication. Yet to abstain from negotiation only intensified an already grim predicament. Every *coup d'état* within France, every inconstancy in the fortunes of war, made sure predictions impossible and the practice of diplomacy was infinitely more complex than Fox's generalisations allowed. The Peace of Amiens, necessary as it was, illustrated the weakness of any settlement without that security which Pitt thought indispensable. Fox's criticisms performed a valuable service. It was important to explore every prospect (however dim) of a diplomatic solution, for if everyone fell into the iron obstinacy of Grenville there could be no way out of the deadlock. Even the brief, twilight peace would have been impossible. But Pitt's caution was well founded: there was no simple formula for easing international tension.

As yet Amiens lay in the future. The failure of Malmesbury's mission made a renewal of full-scale hostilities inevitable. Pitt set about building up another coalition against France. The support of the continental nations was to be guaranteed by the promise of territorial adjustments after the war, and by the payment of large subsidies. Austria would be given Lombardy; the Low Countries would be united to form a barrier against French expansion; the powers would secure the independence of Switzerland. This looked impressive, but victory had still to be won, and without it the scheme would be just another scrap of paper. Bonaparte's star had now risen in the east, where he hoped to establish an empire rivalling that of the British in India. By conquering the Ottomans he would wrest the control of the seas from the stubborn islanders. He defeated the Mamelukes at the battle of the Pyramids, and dabbled in the fascinating curiosities of the Orient, toying with the idea of conversion to Islam. Meanwhile Nelson, after scouring the Mediterranean for the French fleet, found his quarry moored in Aboukir Bay. Defying fortune, the British ships sailed between the French and the coast, subjecting them to a double line of fire. The French flagship *L'Orient* blew up, and only two vessels escaped. The battle of the Nile left Napoleon stranded in Egypt, with an army far from home and cut off from reinforcements. When he tried to break out into Asia he found his way barred at Acre by Sidney Smith and a handful of British sailors, who stiffened the resistance of the Turkish garrison. He had nothing to look forward to but further frustration.

In Europe the Russians under Suvorov, and the Austrians under the Archduke Charles, pressed the French hard. The second coalition seemed about to achieve what had been denied to its predecessor in the summer of 1793. Bonaparte's Italian conquests were lost by the Republic, and Masséna was beleaguered in Switzerland. Although the

Duke of York experienced another disappointing campaign in Holland, where there was little co-operation between the British and Russian forces, allied hopes were high. The Directory, riddled with corruption, seemed about to collapse in disgrace. Many looked to the army for salvation, but Hoche, the anticipated deliverer, died. Bonaparte, learning the plight of France from a newspaper thrown into his camp by Sidney Smith, abandoned his army to its fate and sailed home. On landing he was hailed with enthusiasm, and the *coup d'état* of Brumaire installed him as First Consul. But those who had devised the fall of the Directors had acquired a master, not a servant. In December 1799 Bonaparte made offers of peace. Grenville dissented from the decision to treat, and George III viewed the proceedings with gloomy suspicion: he was convinced of the venality of the French, whom he thought capable of any deceit. Pitt wanted peace, but only if honour could be satisfied and security obtained. Grenville's haughtiness ruined any chance of a settlement, and the year which was to have seen the triumph of the coalition brought only humiliation. Bonaparte, saved at the last moment by Desaix's cavalry charge, defeated the Austrians at Marengo, and though the conquest of Mysore by the future victor of Waterloo soothed English consciences, the defeat of Hohenlinden compelled the Emperor to sue for peace, and to accept the terms of Lunéville. The Russians left the coalition, and with the Danes, Swedes, and Prussians formed the Armed Neutrality of the North, which, like its forerunner during the American War, was directed against the British naval blockade. When Nelson destroyed the Danish fleet at Copenhagen English fortunes in the northern seas were restored. The campaigns had repeated the familiar stalemate: whilst France was supreme on the Continent, Britain remained defiant and invincible at sea. But the Irish rebellion had raised other issues, and although Lake saved Ireland for George III at Vinegar Hill, the King's obduracy forced Pitt to resign before Copenhagen had been won. Men could hardly believe that Pitt was out of office after so many years, that what Fox and his friends had failed to accomplish for so long had been effected by the proposed emancipation of the Catholic peasants of Ireland. In a world reeling with swift and violent change Pitt's fall seemed yet another blow at the old certainties. He had survived the trials of the French Revolution, but, like many other British statesmen, he failed to solve the perennial riddle of Ireland.

5 THE IRISH REBELLION AND UNION, 1798–1801

Long before the Irish rebellion Pitt had experienced the vagaries of politics in that unhappy country. Thwarted over his commercial resolutions in 1785, and defied during the Regency controversy four years later, he knew of the constant struggle between the authorities in Dublin Castle and the intransigent Parliament on College Green. But the crisis of 1798 was more than another squabble between those fortunate enough to share the privilege of political power: the bitterness of Irish politics was equalled only by their complexity. Religious and racial animosity, the memory of ancient wrongs, social injustice, and widespread poverty, were all woven into a terrifying pattern of fear, hatred, and distrust. An aristocratic minority, of mixed English and Irish descent, enjoyed a complete ascendancy in Church and State. Exercising an unlimited influence over the Irish Parliament, and increasingly impatient of subservience to London, they gained legislative independence at the close of the American War. Concerned only with freedom for themselves, and despising both the Catholic peasantry and the northern Dissenters, they luxuriated in the delights of power without responsibility.

But their complacency was soon to be rudely shattered. The majority of Irishmen loathed the Dublin Parliament and administration as the venal representatives of alien rule, for Catholic and Presbyterian alike were excluded from any share in the government of their country. In three out of the four provinces the peasants, cowed but not broken, remained obstinately devoted to the faith of their fathers, whilst in Ulster the Presbyterians bitterly resented their exclusion from an allegedly Protestant establishment. Only after its demise did Grattan's Parliament win a place in the affections of the people.

The French Revolution heralded a new era. Irishmen dreamed of a republic, liberated from the English yoke, which would unite Catholic and Protestant in a common cause. With French assistance Ireland would be free at last, 'from the Shannon to the sea'. The 'United Irishmen' dedicated themselves to the republican ideal: anticipating the struggle for freedom they swore in their followers, intimidating the weak and inciting the strong. Catholic emancipation and Parliamentary reform became the focal-points of controversy, but, while Grattan sought to amend the established order, the United Irishmen rejected it. When his schemes of timely and moderate reform were foiled, the leadership of Irish opinion passed to others, less scrupulous in their patriotism. For all their lauded independence of Westminster the Anglo-Irish were dependent on British arms.

Though Ireland was more prosperous in the years immediately following 1782 than at any other time in the eighteenth century, the major problems of her economy had not been solved. Her lack of mineral resources, industrial weakness, and increasing reliance on the potato were untouched by political innovations. Agricultural development, limited by the natural endowments of the island, was crippled by heavy rents and continued absenteeism amongst the landlords. Nor had the division between the nation and the oligarchy been healed. Catholics and Presbyterians grumbled against the payment of tithes to a church detested by the former as heretical, and by the latter as the preserve of a class. Although the Regency crisis had exposed the deficiencies of the Irish constitution, men remained blind to the dangers of their predicament. Grattan was a sincere patriot, fired by the vision of a free, united Ireland, but his whig preoccupation with curbing the influence of the executive gave the impression of irresponsibility and opportunism, and young men, conscious of the startling achievements which had attended revolutionary violence in France, became impatient with his regard for legality. And, in any event, there was a certain unreality about Grattan's policy. By granting civil rights to the Catholics and Dissenters he hoped to win their goodwill, to make them allies instead of rebels, and by reforming Parliament he sought to transform it into an assembly representative of the nation. 'The Irish Protestant', he boldly declared, 'can never be free until the Irish Catholic has ceased to be a slave.' But nothing was farther from his mind than the destruction of the Protestant ascendancy: the enfranchised were to identify themselves with the existing social structure. Others did not share his sublime confidence. Fitzgibbon, the Irish Chancellor—later created Earl of Clare for his services—thought such a solution impracticable. There would always be two Irelands. The Catholics had to be kept at bay, and to admit them to full citizenship was to flirt with revolution. Even the benevolent distrusted change. Carlisle told Pitt of his misgivings, in a letter which expressed the typical reaction of his class:

> I cannot help looking at that country with a sort of affection, like an old house which one has once inhabited, not disliking the ancient arrangement of its interior, and perhaps unreasonably prejudiced against many of its modern innovations.

Yet, faced with the unrest generated by the French Revolution, even the most rigid conceded the necessity of some measure of conciliation. Irish hopes were raised by the enfranchisement of the Catholic freeholders, and by the relaxation of the regulations governing intermarriage, inheritance, and education—all urged by Pitt on the reluctant and apprehensive administration in Dublin. But these expectations were cruelly dashed by the Fitzwilliam affair, which discredited the government and shook popular faith in the constitutional opposition. Ironically, the accession of the Portland whigs to the ministry seemed to open the way for an improvement in Anglo-Irish relations. Several of the new members of the government had worked with Grattan in the past, and in the autumn of 1794 Pitt had discussions with the Irish leader. He shared his desire for Catholic relief, for he was more concerned with the dangers of radicalism in Ulster than the threat from southern Catholicism. But the emancipation of the Catholics called for careful preparation. The feelings of the Irish aristocracy could not be ignored, and on the religious issue the King required skilful handling. Time, and the painstaking cultivation of every favourable change in the climate of opinion, were indispensable. Therefore, before his departure to assume the Lord-Lieutenancy, Fitzwilliam was warned against the premature agitation of the Catholic question, and the imprudence of introducing official legislation on the subject. He was also instructed not to change the system in Dublin, or to dismiss any office-holder for any reason other than insubordination. Yet no sooner had he landed in Ireland at the beginning of 1795, than he dismissed the Commissioner for Revenue and the Secretary at War. At first Pitt refused to believe the report—'it would be an open breach of a most solemn promise'. But Fitzwilliam did not confine himself to these assertions of his authority. After receiving addresses from both Catholics and Presbyterians he promised full civil equality, bringing in a Bill to that effect on 12 February 1795.

The British Cabinet was acutely embarrassed by the conduct of the Viceroy. The sincerity of Fitzwilliam's actions cannot be impugned, but his impetuosity dealt a severe, if not a mortal, blow to the policies he cherished. It is possible that he was tempted to indulge his own inclinations by the enthusiasm with which he was received in Dublin, but the Cabinet had erred in contenting themselves with a verbal undertaking not to alter the system in Ireland. Fitzwilliam undoubtedly overstepped the bounds of his commission. He had been sent out to prepare the way for emancipation, not to achieve it overnight. George III was indignant. After no more than three weeks in Ireland the Lord-Lieutenant was overturning 'the fabric that the wisdom of our fathers esteemed necessary'. The King lamented that religion was little attended to by persons of rank: toleration—or rather indifference —was too common. But he consoled himself with the thought that the 'bulk of the nation' had not yet been 'spoilt by foreign travels and manners'.

There was no choice in the matter. Pitt could not defy the King, the Anglo-Irish, and a considerable body of opinion at home. The Cabinet was unanimous. Even Fitzwilliam's closest colleagues agreed that he must be recalled. The Irish interpreted the affair as a dishonourable trick. To the Catholics, Fitzwilliam was a deliverer, deserted by an unprincipled and cowardly government. The reckless Earl left Dublin amidst national mourning, and his successor, Lord Camden, was greeted with riots. Pitt hid his disgust under his habitual calm. Fitzwilliam, self-willed if idealistic, had made just the sort of clumsy error which could bring disaster to the minister's plans. The Catholic issue had been trumpeted abroad. The Irish had seen themselves on the threshold of political equality. The oligarchy had been alarmed by the threat of their ascendancy. The King's deepest prejudices had been

inflamed. Emancipation was possible only after consultation, delibera-
tion, the adroit courting of every interested party. Fitzwilliam's
indiscretion imperilled every prospect of relief.

More serious still was the effect of the incident on Irish opinion.
Convinced that they had been duped and betrayed, the Irish turned to
other ways of achieving their freedom, and although Pitt hoped to
conciliate the Catholics by the charter for Maynooth College he was
disappointed. The United Irishmen seized their opportunity. They
were a strangely assorted company, embracing characters as diverse as
the chivalrous and foolhardy Lord Edward Fitzgerald; the ambitious
and embittered Wolfe Tone; the drunken and unreliable Napper
Tandy. Catholic and Protestant were to rise in the common cause.
Arms were distributed in Ulster. The design was Jacobinical, the
purpose a republic on the French model. The soldiers of the atheistic
republic were to liberate 'the holy land of Ireland', and by some
mysterious alchemy the old antagonism between Catholic and Protestant was to be dissolved in the process. The troops who had knocked
the Pope down in Italy were to set him up in Ireland. The confusion of
principle extended to the Catholic clergy. The bishops denounced
violence, and counselled obedience to King George III, but, whilst
many priests warned their flocks of the dangers of Jacobinism, stig-
matising the French as godless infidels, others mingled republican
ferocity with Catholic zeal. Many of the Irish priests had been trained
in France, and though their faith was untainted by the worship of
reason, they had acquired a taste for the Parisian solution to political
problems. Sinister rumours travelled far and wide. Camden warned
the government of the spread of the republican movement, the appeal
of its doctrine, and the tightness of its organisation. Happily for the
authorities, the most significant fact about the United Irishmen was
their lack of unity. The division between Catholic and Protestant was
deep, and more than a few lessons in French metaphysics were necessary to heal old feuds. The rivalry between the Whiteboys and the
Peep o' Day Boys matured through mutual atrocity to that between
Defenders and Orangemen. Dark tales told of an Orange Plot to
exterminate all Catholics, others of a Catholic design to massacre all
Protestants. And, in the revival of religious fanaticism, the aristocracy
saw their salvation.

In Ulster, Lake disarmed the populace with so much brutality that

Abercromby rebuked the troops for their licentiousness: an indiscretion which led to his recall, not to a more humane policy. Whilst the Earl of Moira vainly pleaded the wisdom of emancipation and reform at Dublin and Westminster, O'Connor and O'Coigley conspired to bring French troops to Ireland. But their project was discovered, and its ringleaders arrested. One by one the principal rebels were tracked down. Lord Edward Fitzgerald, seized in a Dublin lodging-house, was wounded while resisting arrest, and died several days later. The search for arms continued, and atrocities were committed without regard to age, sex, or religion. When Grattan and Moira denounced the barbarities endured by the people of Ulster, Camden defended the disarmament on the grounds of necessity. His bland disclaimers were tragically complacent: innocent and guilty alike had been flogged, tortured, hanged. The revolt burst out in full fury in Leinster: Wexford, Carlow, and Wicklow were soon ablaze. But in Ulster the savagery had served its purpose: the risings were feeble. Connaught and Munster were quiet.

Despite all the fine talk of a united Irish republic, the rebellion was almost entirely limited to the Catholic peasantry in one province. The aristocratic and Protestant leaders were either under arrest, dead, or kicking their heels in frustrated anguish in France. The leadership therefore devolved on those priests who were prepared to defy their bishops. The rising soon lost its republican character, and assumed the more familiar shape of a massive agrarian disorder, laced with a strong dash of religious mania. The abolition of tithes and the reduction of rent meant more to the peasants than republican idealism or Irish nationalism. The part played by the Orangemen in quelling the rebellion emphasised the reversion to religious conflict. Under the leadership of fanatical priests the rebels indulged their understandable desire for vengeance. Houses and farms were burnt; Protestant landlords murdered; suspected Orangemen executed; known informers put to death. Both sides accused the other of hideous atrocities; both made these the excuse for the undeniable horrors they inflicted. The insurgents were checked, first at New Ross, then at Arklow. Finally Lake stormed the principal rebel camp at Vinegar Hill, and though spasmodic fighting continued, that was really the end. Father Michael Murphy, whom the ignorant peasants believed invulnerable to Protestant bullets, had been blown to pieces by canister shot. Father John

Murphy, who had boasted that he could catch bullets in his hand, was hanged. Father Kearns, whose vast weight had saved his life in Paris during the reign of terror by bending the lamp-post on which he had been strung up, did not escape the rope. For the rank and file retribution was still more cruel. The deluded peasants, who had trusted in sacred medals to save them from shot and shell, were pursued with vindictive savagery. The yeomanry and militia raped with impunity, executed without trial, and perfected the prolonged agony of the pitched cap. Licence took the place of law, and the outrages which had accompanied the rising gave ample encouragement to bigoted officials who dwelt freely on the dangers of giving civil rights to Catholics.

In August, General Humbert landed with 1100 French troops in County Mayo, but, although he put the forces which met him to flight at the Castlebar races, he was compelled to surrender at Ballinamuck. In October, Wolfe Tone was captured on board a French man-of-war in Lough Swilly. A month later he was tried in Dublin, bravely defending his conduct in court:

> From my earliest youth I have regarded the connexion between Ireland and Great Britain as the curse of the Irish nation, and felt convinced that, while it lasted, this country would never be free or happy. My mind has been confirmed in this opinion by the experience of every succeeding year.

After his request to be shot had been refused, he committed suicide in prison. Defiant to the end, he joined the ranks of the Irish martyrs, and his words echoed down the nineteenth century to take on new significance in the twentieth.

The rebellion, rich in heroism as well as crime, had accomplished nothing. Instead of healing the feud between Catholic and Protestant it had exacerbated it, and a united Ireland was as far away as ever. In Ulster the Orange lodges ousted the republican movement, which became increasingly Catholic in temperament. For Pitt, the cautious advocate of reform and relief, the rebellion was a disaster. Emancipation was doubly suspect, and unless there was a drastic change in the constitutional relationship between the two kingdoms, it would be impossible to guide the King, the Anglo-Irish, and the English conservatives, along the road to enlightenment. The war had revealed England's weakness, and as long as it lasted the Irish would be tempted to rebel, the French to invade. A practical solution to the Irish problem had to be found.

Thoughts turned to legislative union. Cornwallis—whose dis-approval of the brutalities permitted, if not promoted, by Lake, had earned him harsh criticism from the Irish aristocrats—was convinced that it was the answer. Pitt had never regarded the suppression of the rebellion as more than a preliminary to amelioration and reform. His sympathies lay with the Catholics, and he had already seen his attempts to relieve Ireland's woes frustrated by interests too strong to be ignored, and too obtuse to be persuaded. The idea of Union had been in the back of his mind for some years. In 1792 he had broached the subject with Westmorland, then Lord-Lieutenant, but he had no illusions—'it must certainly require great delicacy and management'. Once Union was accomplished, emancipation would become feasible, for the Protes-tant ascendancy would not then be endangered. Pitt remembered Adam Smith's advocacy of a political Union between Britain and Ireland, and he was heartened by the example of the Union with Scotland, which had been beneficial to both countries. For Pitt, Union and Emancipation were one policy, and although the Union of the Parliaments is now seen in the light of the tragic experience of the nineteenth and twentieth centuries, had emancipation been granted in 1801, without the bad feeling and agitation which led up to the conces-sion in 1829, the story might have been very different. The respon-sibility for the failure of the experiment does not lie with Pitt, but with those who preferred to drive him from office, rather than implement a policy upon which he had set his heart.

Union was imperative if emancipation was ever to be achieved. Many supported Union in the hope of evading emancipation. Lough-borough and Clare loathed the thought of civil equality for the Catholics, yet both were convinced that legislative Union was neces-sary. The King saw the advantages of Union, but remained opposed to emancipation. His distracted mind was obsessed with his coronation oath. When his dim vision was clouded by conscientious scruples, no persuasion could shake his mulish resolve, and Pitt was over-sanguine in his confidence that, given time, he could bring George III round. It would be difficult enough getting the Union through the Irish Parlia-ment. Although the aristocracy relied on the British connection for the maintenance of their monopoly, they clung to their illusory independence with a tenacity remarkable in its indifference to facts. How much more hateful a political union would be, which gave full citizenship to the Catholics!

Pitt's every action was open to misrepresentation, and while he had no doubt that both Union and Emancipation were necessary, he could not afford to let this be known before the first had been carried out. He had to persuade the Anglo-Irish to give up their Parliament, and then to convince the united Parliament and the King of the wisdom of Emancipation. To accomplish this would tax his considerable skill in moving, step by step, towards political objectives.

When the news of his intentions leaked in Dublin first reactions were unfavourable. The Dublin Bar condemned any tampering with legislative independence, and shoals of pamphlets were published against the Union. The opposition was stronger than Cornwallis, the Lord-Lieutenant, realised. When the government's proposals were debated in the Irish Parliament in January 1799 an amendment, calling for the retention of an independent legislature, was defeated by only one vote. Pitt was disappointed, but, grieved though he was that a measure essential to the welfare of both countries might be balked by 'prejudice and cabal', he pressed on with his scheme. The reception given to the proposal to unite the Parliaments reminded him of the need to hold his peace about emancipation until the imperial legislature was in being.

On 31 January 1800 he outlined the reasons for Union in an eloquent speech in the House of Commons. Ireland was the vulnerable spot in the United Kingdom, and in wartime the existence of separate legislatures was potentially dangerous. He referred to the religious troubles which bedevilled Irish life, and affirmed that an establishment representing a minority was far different from one reflecting the religion of the majority of a people. Yet, while Ireland remained politically independent, full concessions to the Catholics would undermine the constitution. (Here was a hint that, after Union, some accommodation with the Catholics was possible, but it was not a formal pledge. Pitt never forgot that he was dealing with Parliamentary assemblies; that patience, resource, and sheer drudgery would be needed to persuade bitter enemies to accede to his solution of the problem.) An imperial legislature would be able to consider the issue of emancipation with a vision and far-sightedness denied to the local Parliament in Dublin. If the privileges of citizenship were withheld from the Catholics for a time, many of their grievances would, none the less, be mitigated by the Union. Pitt was not committing himself to a modern party programme. He was interested in practical results, not public slogans. It would take time to induce those who had grudgingly given up their independence to perceive the necessity of emancipation.

There was only one way of dealing with the Irish magnates. An appeal would have to be made to their self-interest. Pitt had been willing to pay compensation to the British borough-mongers; now, faced with an even more stubborn resistance by those who felt their property rights threatened, he used the same form of persuasion. Seven thousand pounds were offered for each borough, and the lavish distribution of sinecures, patronage, and titles helped the irresolute to make up their minds. For this Pitt has been condemned, and the means by which the Dublin Parliament was prevailed upon to end its own existence have been used to blacken the Union and to discredit the minister and his associates—Cornwallis, Castlereagh, and Clare. Yet it is difficult to see what else could have been done. Rational arguments were not enough. Whatever theories one may hold on Parliamentary democracy, in the eighteenth century seats in Parliament were regarded as pieces of private property. By the standards of the time it was thought monstrous to deprive a man of his property without paying him for it. Twentieth-century expropriation would have appeared as immoral to Pitt as the use of bribery and influence is offensive to modern sensitivities. If the Union was necessary, then the means were justified. They were the usual methods, an integral part of the contemporary political mechanism. When so many men went into Parliament simply because it was the thing to do, they had to be compensated for the loss in social prestige incurred with the disappearance of their seats. And, whatever disappointments the Catholics experienced after 1800, they had nothing to hope for from the Dublin Parliament. Notoriously corrupt, even by contemporary standards, it had been the agent of a narrow and obscurantist oligarchy, and it was fitting that it should close its career amidst unparalleled bribery.

Cornwallis and Castlereagh were disgusted with their task, despite its inevitability. They performed it with the stoical diligence of men who knew that they were doing their duty. Only this sustained them in their constant encounter with avarice and greed. Grubby bargaining for a higher price overruled objections to amalgamation with the British legislature.

But opposition to the Union was not limited to Ireland. Fox was absent from the Commons, but his abhorrence of the measure was common knowledge. Grey and Sheridan both spoke against the Bill, the latter with all the dedication of the expatriate. But the ministry gradually gained the upper hand. The Irish members were slowly won over. Cornwallis had also been courting the Catholics, and Castlereagh was convinced that a majority of them favoured Union. Meanwhile, the price for boroughs was raised to £15,000, and a total of £1,260,000 was spent in compensation. Forty-six promotions in the peerage and twenty ecclesiastical appointments helped to sway the issue. Four thousand guineas were paid for a single vote. In the spring of 1800 the Dublin Parliament approved the Union: at Westminster the resolutions were passed by a large majority. But emancipation, the prospect of which had secured much Catholic sympathy for the measure, had still to be attained.

Pitt was now to experience disappointment, all the more painful because it was tinged with treachery. The King was still brooding over his coronation oath. His mind, increasingly prone to attacks of insanity, had not been set at rest by assurances that the repeal of the Test Act would not constitute a breach of his solemn promise. His anxiety was heightened by Loughborough, the Lord Chancellor, who had taken the opportunity, when the King was holidaying at Weymouth, to whisper in his ear that repeal would infringe the oath, and that the ministry was contemplating this drastic step. He did not tell his colleagues of what he had done. The King's prejudices were now at their most violent, and the Archbishop of Canterbury stiffened his sovereign's determination by denouncing Catholic relief. In September 1800 Loughborough showed the King a letter from Pitt summoning him to a Cabinet at which the Catholic question was to be discussed. George III assumed that his ministers were engaged in some dark conspiracy, and his Protestant convictions were intensified by his fears of what the government intended to do.

In fact, the ministers wished to substitute a political test for the out-moded religious requirement. An oath was to be imposed, pledging the maintenance of the constitution in Church and State. Catholics would be admitted to public life, but they would have to accept the

Protestant establishment. Loughborough opposed this suggestion in the Cabinet, and Pitt, who wanted to have the matter settled in every particular before approaching the King, postponed further discussion for three months. He was in poor health throughout the autumn of 1800, and spent several weeks convalescing with the Addington family near Reading. But Loughborough had not been idle. Instead of thinking things over in calm and seclusion he whipped up the King's anxieties to a greater pitch, and when deliberations were resumed in the new year he remained obdurate. Worse still, the weaker members of the ministry became acutely sensitive to the difficulties which had to be overcome. Westmorland opposed emancipation with the authority of a former Lord-Lieutenant; Liverpool went over; Portland wavered; Pitt's brother, the Earl of Chatham, joined the opposition to Catholic relief.

The unsuspicious Pitt was soon to learn the public consequences of Loughborough's perfidy. The King behaved with appalling violence at the levee on 28 January. He talked of Castlereagh in ominous terms —'What is it that this young Lord has brought over which they are going to throw at my head?'—and called emancipation 'the most Jacobinical thing' he'd ever heard of. Then he took up a familiar line: 'I shall reckon any man my personal enemy who proposes any such measure.' The next day Addington was told to 'open Mr. Pitt's eyes to the danger . . . which may prevent his even speaking to me on a subject upon which I can scarcely keep my temper'. The situation was grave.

On the last day of January, Pitt wrote to the King, lucidly expounding the necessity of affording some relief to the Catholics, and politely indicating that he could not continue in office unless this was granted:

> Mr. Pitt . . . trusts your Majesty will believe that every principle of duty, gratitude, and attachment must make him look to your Majesty's ease and satisfaction. . . . Under the impression of that opinion, he has concurred in what appeared to be the prevailing sentiments of the majority of the Cabinet—that the admission of the Catholics and Dissenters to offices, and of the Catholics to Parliament . . . would, under certain conditions . . . be highly advisable, with a view to the tranquillity and improvement of Ireland, and to the general interest of the United Kingdom. For himself, he is . . . convinced that the measure would be attended with no danger to the Established Church, or to the Protestant interest in Great Britain or Ireland. . . . That the grounds on which the laws of exclusion . . . were founded, have long been narrowed, and are since the Union removed. . . .

Pitt argued that the new oath would be more effective than the
religious test, and that the payment of the Irish clergy by the State
would reconcile them to the government. He continued:

> Mr. Pitt humbly conceives a new security might be obtained for the Civil
> and Ecclesiastical Constitution of this country, more applicable to the
> present circumstances, more free from objection, and more effectual in
> itself, than any which now exists; and which would at the same time admit
> of extending such indulgences as must conciliate the higher orders of the
> Catholics, and by furnishing to a large class of your Majesty's Irish subjects
> a proof of the goodwill of the United Parliament, afford the best chance of
> giving full effect to the great object of the Union—that of tranquillising
> Ireland, and attaching it to this country.

Pitt went out of his way to soothe the injured feelings of the King,
promising to refrain from raising the issue in Parliament while
George III considered his proposals. But he was firm in his belief that
emancipation was sufficiently serious to merit his resignation if it was
rejected:

> If . . . your Majesty's objections to the measure proposed should not be
> removed, or sufficiently diminished to admit of its being brought forward
> with your Majesty's full concurrence, and with the whole weight of
> Government, it must be personally Mr. Pitt's first wish to be released from
> a situation which he is conscious that, under such circumstances, he could
> not continue to fill but with the greatest disadvantage.

He was willing to stay in office until alternative arrangements had been
made, but, though he had no desire to embarrass either the King or the
new administration by the continued agitation of the Catholic question,
his decision was final. He ended by

> submitting to your Majesty the indispensable necessity of effectually dis-
> countenancing . . . all attempts to make use of your Majesty's name, or to
> influence the opinion of any individual, or descriptions of men, on any
> part of this subject.

The letter was calm, dignified, and respectful. Even the threat to
resign was veiled in modest language. Pitt was showing his usual
regard for the accepted conventions of the constitution. He saw that it
would be improper for him to impose his will upon the King, and
recognised the impossibility of doing so. He hoped to humour

George III by stressing the way in which the government's proposals would strengthen the established order. But all was of no avail.

On the following day the King replied. He was unshakeable in his detestation of relief for the Catholics. Religious, as well as political, duty made it imperative that those holding high office in the State should receive the sacrament according to the Anglican rite. He had held these opinions for forty years, and he would never change them. But he promised to abstain from talking about the subject—'the one nearest my heart'—adding, 'I cannot help it if others pretend to guess at my opinions, which I have never disguised.' His affection for Pitt helped him to put this restraint upon himself, but he insisted that those who supported the measure should also remain silent.

> Though I do not pretend to have the power of changing Mr. Pitt's opinion, when thus unfortunately fixed, yet I shall hope his sense of duty will prevent his retiring from his present situation to the end of my life; for I can with great truth assert that I shall, from public and private considerations, feel great regret if I shall ever find myself obliged at any time, from a sense of religious and political duty, to yield to his entreaties of retiring from his seat at the Board of the Treasury.

The old man had lost none of his cunning. On 31 January he had approached Addington about the formation of a new ministry—'Where am I to turn for support if *you* do not stand by me?' Though he wanted Pitt to stay in office, George III was in a position to dictate his terms. He was calling what he hoped was Pitt's bluff. Faced with the King's unflinching negative, Pitt had no choice. On 3 February he again wrote to his master:

> The final decision which your Majesty has formed on the great subject in question . . . and Mr. Pitt's own unalterable sense of the line which public duty requires from him, must make him consider the moment as now arrived when . . . it must be his first wish to be released as soon as possible from his present situation. . . .

In March, Addington took office at the head of a new ministry.

Pitt has been accused of mishandling the affair, but it is difficult to see how George III's opposition could have been overcome. Pitt had hoped to confront the King with proposals which had the backing of a united Cabinet, but his colleagues were divided and hesitant, and the attitude of the Commons was doubtful. He was no modern party leader, with an obedient phalanx of voters at his command. He could not survive if he offended both King and Commons, and accepting as he did the contemporary interpretation of the relationship between monarch and minister, he had no inclination to force the King to consent to his solution, even had he been in a position to do so. His resignation was as ineffective as it was necessary. Emancipation had been implied in much that he had said, and although no formal promise had been given he was committed to the Catholic cause. Yet he had no intention of entering upon systematic opposition. Such conduct was foreign to his concept of constitutional practice. But, while contemporaries thought that Pitt made too much of the Catholic issue, historians have suggested that he left office because the coalition had failed, and because a negotiation with Bonaparte was inevitable. To argue thus is to ignore the fact that Pitt had never agreed with Burke and Windham: he had been prepared to negotiate with the Directory, and despite his disappointment with the outcome of his efforts to create an invincible alliance he never shrank from looking reality in the face. His support for Addington over the Peace of Amiens indicates that he realised some pause in the hostilities was desirable. He would not have made an inferior negotiator, and instead of avoiding all responsibility for the peace he expressly approved it. On 29 October 1801 he told the Commons of his satisfaction with the preliminaries:

> Whatever criticism may be applied to inferior parts of these great transactions, they are on the whole such as afford great joy to the country, and entitle the Government which concluded them to esteem and thanks.

In the debate of 3 November he again supported the government, although the peace had not fulfilled his expectations. But, nevertheless,

> we have the satisfaction of knowing that we have survived the violence of the revolutionary fever, and that we have seen the extent of its principles abated. We have seen Jacobinism deprived of its fascination; we have seen it stripped of the name and pretence of liberty. It has shown itself to be capable only of destroying, not of building, and with a military despotism as its necessary end.

Yet he ended on an ominous note—'I am inclined to hope everything that is good. But I am bound to act as if I feared otherwise.'

Before Pitt had ceased to be minister, and while arrangements were still being made for Addington to take over, George III went mad. The strain of the Catholic controversy culminated in mental breakdown. The King said that he would rather beg from door to door than violate his coronation oath, and told his family that if he broke his word he would no longer be the nation's legal sovereign. Pitt decided to follow the precedent of 1788, but, before he could introduce a Bill setting up a limited Regency, the King recovered at the beginning of March 1801. No sooner had he been restored to his senses than he sent a message to Pitt: 'Tell him I am now quite well—quite recovered from my illness; but what has *he* not to answer for who is the cause of my having been ill at all?' George III had a gift for a species of persuasion which hovered unhealthily between blackmail and a naïve appeal to good will. The members of the Cabinet were hurt and distressed by what had passed, and though Pitt was too proud to parade his feelings, he was deeply wounded by the suggestion that he was responsible for the King's collapse. Before laying down the burdens of government, he promised that he would never raise the Catholic issue during George III's lifetime. It was impossible to wage a campaign on behalf of the Catholics, with the danger of insanity looming in the background. Few men wanted to run the risk of Regency, when this meant the installation of Fox and the opposition whigs—men despised by many of their countrymen as fellow-travellers and Jacobin sympathisers. The King's prejudices were part of the price which had to be paid for a sovereign who did more than reign. George III was a constitutional monarch, and as such he played a real part in the government of the country. But he was now in his sixties, and his health was failing. If Catholic emancipation had to wait, would it have to wait for long? The pledge for which Pitt has been so harshly condemned was given, in turn, by Castlereagh and Tierney in 1803, Canning in 1804, even by Fox and Grenville in 1806. The same justification can be pleaded in each case: there was no prospect of carrying the measure as long as George III lived. The promise, decisive though it sounds, did little more than recognise known political realities.

So, on 14 March 1801, Pitt retired from the Treasury after seventeen arduous years. Cornwallis and Castlereagh in Ireland, Grenville, Dundas, Spencer, and Windham in England, followed his example. Portland, Chatham, and Westmorland remained. But though Addington's ministry was weak in debate, it had the confidence of the war-weary back-benchers, who distrusted Pitt over the Catholic question, and who were not a little relieved to have a government free from the embarrassment of genius. Addington's unimaginative common sense reflected their own feelings. Meanwhile Pitt gave the ministry general support as a private Member. In March 1802, after peevish negotiations, the Peace of Amiens was signed. Addington's desire for peace had been so strong that he had abandoned Pitt's demands. Britain restored all her conquests to France and her satellites, with the exception of Ceylon and Trinidad, and she also undertook to return Malta to the Knights of St. John. The French promised to withdraw from Naples, Central Italy, and the Papal States, and it was hoped that the guarantees of independence given by France to the republics in Holland, Switzerland, and northern Italy would be honoured. These were confirmed by the Treaty of Lunéville, to which Britain was not a party, but suspicions of French good faith on these matters made Malta the technical reason for the renewal of the war. As yet, that lay in the future. The armistice was fun while it lasted. British tourists went to Paris to see the sights, even to peep at the man whose name was used to frighten badly behaved children. When the attempt to live amicably with the new order failed, men were all the more convinced that the rapacity of the French was insatiable, that the British cause was just, and that only the defeat of Bonaparte could secure liberty and a lasting peace.

6 THE LAST PHASE, 1801–1806

FOR three years Pitt was free from the anxieties of office, but his retirement brought him little ease. Politics became increasingly bitter as relations with France worsened, and as confidence in the Addington ministry waned. But, while the opposition splintered into several irreconcilable factions, Pitt remained aloof. As long as Addington commanded a majority in the Commons, and retained the approval of the King, he felt bound by his promise of general support. He wished to return to office in response to national feeling, not in consequence of a sustained onslaught on the minister. His reticence earned him the criticism of friend and foe. To many of his disciples it seemed that he valued his own honour more than the country's safety. Only as the drift into war continued, and as he became more apprehensive about Addington's fiscal policy and the state of the national defences, did he move over to the offensive. The complicated political manœuvres which marked the last year of the Addington interlude ensured that Pitt's second ministry would not be the broadly based, patriotic government for which he had hoped. He resumed responsibility for the direction of the war without many of his old colleagues, as well as without the whigs, and wits soon talked of the ministry of Billy and Pitt.

He enjoyed life at Walmer Castle, spending much of his time riding, shooting, sailing, and farming, but he also faced financial ruin, bereavement, and illness. His debts were estimated at little less than £50,000, and, since he obdurately refused to accept anything from the public, he was saved from his creditors only by the kindness of friends. Determined not to lay himself open to the charge that his conduct was influenced by private obligation, rather than public policy, he had rejected offers of help from George III and £100,000 from the merchants of London. But his old tutor, Pretyman, the Bishop of Lincoln (who had now taken the name of Tomline) persuaded him to accept £11,700, which had been collected privately among his friends, and this paid the most urgent debts. Yet Pitt's independence exacted a high price. His resources were so strained that it was necessary for him to part with Holwood, which he sold to Sir George Pocock in 1802. The loss of his country house was a keen disappointment: ever since he had gone bird-nesting at Holwood as a boy he had longed to call the place his own.

His year in frustrated isolation was saddened by the death of his mother in April 1803. He had always been a loving and dutiful son, and he talked frankly to George Rose of the feelings roused by his mother's passing. She was buried beside her husband in Westminster Abbey: before three years had passed, Pitt himself was to rest within the same tomb.

His health had been precarious since 1797. Now it broke down. It was as if the respite from public duty relaxed an inner tension which had sustained him through so many trials. He was tormented by gout and dogged by sickness. In the autumn of 1802 he was seriously ill, and in October he went to Bath, where he took a turn for the better. Besides taking the waters he dieted carefully. He had no lunch, but ate a good dinner, contenting himself with two glasses of madeira during the meal, and restricting himself to less than a pint of port afterwards. He was said to be 'positively in the best possible train of management for his health'. But early in 1803 he was again troubled by gout and persistent bilious attacks. Visits to Bath became a regular restorative. In March, however, Dundas thought Pitt 'much improved in point of health', and in November he was in excellent spirits. But his recovery was deceptive. Throughout the last two years of his life he taxed his physical powers far beyond their strength. When he immersed himself in the toils of the second ministry his constitution was already undermined, and, under the tragic reverses of the coalition, it collapsed. He was in no condition to endure continuous strain. Lady

Hester Stanhope has left a characteristically colourful account of her uncle's exertions:

> What a life was his! Roused from sleep (for he was a good sleeper) with a despatch from Lord Melville; then down to Windsor; then, if he had half an hour to spare, trying to swallow something; Mr. Adams with a paper, Mr. Long with another; then Mr. Rose: then, with a little bottle of cordial confection in his pocket, off to the House until three or four in the morning; then home to a hot supper . . . to talk over what was to be done next day:—and wine, and wine. Scarcely up next morning, when 'tat-tat-tat', twenty or thirty people one after another, and the horses walking before the door from two until sunset, waiting for him. It was enough to kill a man—it was murder.

The state of his health contributed to his political hesitancy. His caution was not shared by his friends. Canning ridiculed the government in acid verses. The public were urged to sing the statesman whom moderate talents had raised to fame, and reminded that

> Pitt is to Addington,
> As London is to Paddington.

The resumption of the war, and the erection of blockhouses on the banks of the Thames, inspired further sarcasms:

> If blocks can from danger deliver,
>   Two places are safe from the French:
> The one is the mouth of the river,
>   The other the Treasury bench.

Canning, Tomline, and Rose all sought to induce Pitt to withhold his support from Addington. The Bishop of Lincoln denounced the conciliatory spirit which Pitt had shown towards his successor. He impressed upon him what he owed to his country, and pointed out that his enemies were sparing no pains to lower him in the public esteem. Tomline believed that Pitt was coming round to the necessity of opposing the ministry, but on the Catholic issue their conversations had been less reassuring. Pitt still looked forward to the time when emancipation could be carried, and Tomline sadly commented: 'I fear he does not wish to take office again unless he could be permitted to bring it forward, and to be properly supported.' On the Catholic question Pitt and his followers were as divided as ever.

On 28 May 1802 a tumultuous banquet was held in the Merchant

Taylors' Hall in celebration of Pitt's birthday. But the hero of the
occasion was conspicuously absent, and in one sense the Pittites were
making a gesture against their master's reserve, as well as paying him
a tribute. When the assembled company bellowed Canning's famous
lines, they were prophesying that the whirlwind had not blown itself
out, as well as commending Pitt's statesmanship:

> And, oh, if again the next tempest should rise,
> The dawnings of peace fresh darkness deform,
> When we turn to thy hopeless retirement our eyes,
> We shall long for the Pilot who weathered the Storm.

And Pitt, likewise, was pessimistic about the future. He did not regret
his defence of the peace, for a breathing-space—however brief—had
been necessary. But it was imperative that Britain should be prepared,
that Bonaparte should understand that there would be no tame submis-
sion to insult or injury. From his retreat at Walmer, Pitt saw the sky
darken and the war-clouds gather.

Whilst Bonaparte fretted at the liberty granted to the British Press—
he did not share the opinion that he was a suitable target for humour
—there were more serious differences between the two powers whose
representatives had so lately signed the peace treaty. The ink on the
parchment was scarcely dry, before the Consul annexed Piedmont and
Elba, and, declaring himself 'Mediator of the Swiss Republic', marched
his troops into Switzerland. French troops also remained in northern
Italy, where the Cisalpine Republic conveniently asked Napoleon to
become President. Holland was unmistakably a puppet State. The spirit,
if not the letter, of the Amiens agreement had been broken. Pitt warned
Addington of the need for 'a very increased and constant preparation', both
naval and military'. His friends pressed on impatiently with schemes to
change the administration. Canning organised an address, urging
Addington to hand over to Pitt, but Pitt opposed the project. Such a
measure, arranged by persons known to be attached to himself, would
look like a plot:

> Whether I really did, or did not, know of it, there would most certainly
> be the suspicion that I had at least connived: and such suspicion, indepen-
> dent of my feelings, would defeat the end of my coming into office, even
> supposing that any good could result from it. It is therefore my wish—one
> which I expressed to Canning before he left Bath, and in which, on
> reflection, I have been confirmed more and more—that no further canvass

should be made for names, supporters, or signatures, to promote or compel
Mr. Addington's resignation. If my coming into office is as generally
desired as you suppose it, it is much better for me, and for the thing itself,
to leave that opinion to work out its own way; and this must happen if
the opinion is a prevailing one in the public mind; and if it is not, my
coming into office at all is useless and improper.

Pitt clung tenaciously to his political neutrality whilst the dispute
with Bonaparte over Malta assumed ominous proportions, and the
publication of Sébastiani's Egyptian report stirred suspicions of French
designs in the east. In Paris, Lord Whitworth, the British ambassador,
was publicly humiliated, the Consul abusing him in language reminis-
cent of the barrack square. The outbreak of war seemed imminent and
inevitable. Bonaparte would strike at any vulnerable point: there was
no time to lose in putting the nation's defences in good order.

But, although many looked to the man whose courage had never
faltered during the darkest days of the Revolutionary War, Pitt underestimated the hostility entertained by many of his friends for Addington.
The more moderate Pittites waited for their leader to make the first
move, but others like Canning fumed at his restraint. Grenville
declined to sit in any Cabinet which included Addington, and refused
to compromise on the Catholic issue. Addington recognised the need
to bring Pitt into the ministry, but shrank from tendering his own
resignation. He contemplated sharing the Secretaryships with Pitt,
Chatham taking over as First Lord of the Treasury, but Pitt scornfully
rejected such a proposal. 'Really,' he said afterwards, 'I had not the
curiosity to ask what I was to be.' When he suggested that the minister
should retire gracefully to the Lords, Addington countered by for-
bidding the accession of Grenville, Windham, and Spencer to the
administration. The negotiations, never very promising, collapsed.
Pitt returned to Walmer, while George III complained that plots were
being hatched to put the Crown in commission. In his contempt for
Addington, Grenville was now edging towards an understanding with
Fox, who only two years before had confessed that he found it difficult
to disguise his pleasure at the triumph of the French. Fox believed that
if war came the responsibility would rest with the British government.
And the quarrel over Malta had now reached deadlock. The British,
disturbed by French aggressions in Europe, would not evacuate the
island: Bonaparte insisted on the terms of the peace treaty. Neither side

gave way, and in May 1803 war was declared. The Consul immediately
shocked civilised opinion by interning all British travellers unfortunate
enough to find themselves stranded in France. The Addington ministry,
so recently the blind advocates of disarmament, hoped for a cheap,
unspectacular, defensive campaign.

To meet the threat of invasion, the government encouraged the
recruitment of local volunteer regiments, and, while the Army of
England gathered on the hills above Boulogne, Pitt became a Colonel
in the Kentish Association. As Warden of the Cinque Ports he took
his military duties seriously. Lady Hester Stanhope marvelled at his
enthusiasm:

> Pitt absolutely goes through the fatigue of the drill sergeant. It is parade
> after parade at fifteen or twenty minutes distance from each other. I often
> attend him; and it is quite as much as I am equal to, although I am remark-
> ably well just now. The hard riding I do not mind, but to remain almost
> *still* so many hours on horseback is an incomprehensible bore, and requires
> more patience than you can easily imagine. . . . If Mr. Pitt does not . . .
> injure his health every other consideration becomes trifling. . . .

But, however vigorous Pitt's interest in military training, contemporaries knew that his talents were better suited to graver responsibilities. The Addington ministry was as supine in war as it had been dull
in peace. Yet, when he returned to the Commons in May 1803, after
a year's absence, Pitt refrained from a direct attack on the government
and defended the justice of the war in a thrilling speech. His reappear-
ance made a great impression on the House: many new Members were
seeing him for the first time. When he entered the chamber all eyes
were fixed upon him. His name was repeated in a universal murmur.
When he rose, there were cries of 'Mr. Pitt! Mr. Pitt!' and before he
said a word he was greeted with tumultuous cheers. When he sat down
the galleries echoed with enthusiastic applause. But a gaunt spectre
haunted his triumph: his voice had lost none of its harmony, but
his breathing was laboured, and it was noted that he was in poor
health.

In June, Pitt tried to protect the ministry from a vote of censure.
Afterwards he confessed that his tactics had been ill-advised. His
attempt to weld together all parties in the national cause had failed.
Grenville, now in fully fledged alliance with Fox, was convinced that
a regular opposition to the ministry was 'an indispensable duty' as the

Treasury. — Mr Pitt

Secretaries of State { Lord Melville
Mr Fox
L. Fitzwilliam

Admiralty — L. Spencer

L. President — L. Grenville

Privy Seal — — D. of Portland

L. Chancellor Lord Eldon

M. General of Ordnance — L. Chatham

Chancellor of Duchy Mr Windham

Board of Controll — L. Castlereagh

Lord Steward. — L. Camden

Committee of Trade — L. Harrowby.

Secy at War — Mr Grey.

Secy to Ireland — = Mr Canning

22 Pitt's proposal, in his own hand, for the constitution of an all-party Cabinet
in May 1804.

first step towards a new government comprehending all men of ability. The prevailing uncertainty was heightened by George III's bout of madness in February 1804: the complexities of a Regency seemed about to be added to the dangers of invasion. But Pitt was now profoundly alarmed by the government's naval policy, and in April—although no formal coalition had been made—he and Fox both voted against the Irish Militia Bill. The government had a majority of twenty-one, but Addington's days were numbered. At the end of the month he resigned, despite the King's pleas that he should stay. Pitt was asked to form a ministry.

He tried to create an all-party Cabinet, but, when he named Fox as Foreign Secretary, he encountered the opposition of the King, whose enfeebled mind boggled at the thought of taking his old enemy into his councils. George III was beyond rational argument: Pitt wryly commented that never in his life had the King so baffled him. Fox, reconciled after a lifetime to the enmity of the King, told his friends to take office without him. Pitt was willing to give them a fair share of posts in the new administration, but, out of personal loyalty to Fox, they refused. Grenville, as faithful to his new ally as he had been to his old, rejected his cousin's proposals. Pitt's reaction was characteristic: 'I will teach that proud man, that in the service, and with the confidence, of the King, I can do without him, though I think my health such that it may cost me my life.' The King talked of regaining an old friend, but his obstinacy had wrecked all hope of a national government.

Meanwhile Napoleon, now Emperor of the French and murderer of the Duc d'Enghien, assembled his Grand Army for the descent upon England. Medals celebrating the conquest were thoughtfully struck beforehand. The French fleets were to evade the blockade, unite in the Atlantic, and seize control of the Channel for long enough to allow the vast armada of transports to be ferried across. However scornful Napoleon was of the ditch separating him from his most stubborn foes, the storm-tossed British fleets still stood between him and the domination of the world.

To break the stalemate Pitt endeavoured to form another military coalition against the French. The surest defence was to strike a decisive blow on land, but for this allies were indispensable, and despite their experience of Napoleon's ruthless brilliance, the old monarchies had learnt little. The coalition was built up painfully slowly. Prussia stayed on the alert for the greatest gain at the slightest risk, leaning now to an English alliance, then to an understanding with the French. But Austria and Russia were more concerned with the French menace, and more amenable to British persuasion. Pitt had matured as a war leader. He had benefited from the mistakes of the 'nineties. Even in the face of invasion he sought to take the offensive by exploiting British sea power to further a great continental war. From this point of view Trafalgar was the climax of an offensive campaign. The strategic centre for Pitt's plans lay in the Mediterranean, where by co-operating with the Russians he hoped to bring the French to battle in Italy. Even after Villeneuve burst into the Atlantic, Pitt did not lose sight of the overall objective. He had brought a new urgency to the direction of the British war effort, as Nelson realised:

> It is, as Mr. Pitt knows, annihilation that the country wants, and not merely a splendid victory . . . honourable to the parties concerned, but absolutely useless in the extended scale to bring Bonaparte to his marrow bones.

Pitt remembered the long, protracted agony of the struggle against the French in the last decade of the eighteenth century. He was impatient for a decision. Perhaps the knowledge that his own health was failing, that his life hung on a thread, spurred him on to seek a speedy conclusion to the war. He no longer relied on economic exhaustion to reduce the French. He had grasped that Napoleon could only be defeated where he was strongest—in the field—and that British sea power could forge an alliance which would compel Napoleon to commit his armies where the allies chose. These were the schemes which dominated Pitt's thinking. In conception his strategy was trenchant, arresting in its boldness. In execution, only the British navy, ably directed by the aged Barham from the Admiralty, lived up to the grandeur of the conception. The armies of the coalition were no match for Napoleon's swift columns, and no amount of insight on Pitt's part could compensate for the fatal lethargy which afflicted allied generalship. Instead of destroying the French Emperor, Pitt's grand strategy brought its author to his grave.

Yet, although he failed to win the final victory for which he craved, Pitt thwarted Napoleon's plans to invade England. Nelson chased

Villeneuve across the Atlantic, discovering on his return that after an indecisive battle off Cape Finisterre, the French had taken refuge in Cadiz. Napoleon, infuriated by the failure of his admirals to apply a strategy which had seemed irresistible in the map-rooms of Paris, branded Villeneuve as a coward. Determined to strike at his continental enemies before their preparations were complete, he broke camp at Boulogne. But, while he marched off to the glories of Ulm and Austerlitz, he had provoked Trafalgar. Villeneuve, stung by the slur on his honour and the news that he was to be superseded, gave battle. The Spanish and French fleets, exposed to the Nelson touch, were overwhelmingly defeated. Two-thirds of their ships were taken, and Napoleon's naval power destroyed, but Nelson's death dimmed the nation's joy at the greatest of his victories. Pitt, who had attended the admiral to his carriage on his last visit to Downing Street, was awakened with the news. His habitual ability to sleep deserted him, and he rose at three in the morning to work off his mingled exhilaration and distress. But the coalition fared as disastrously as Napoleon's invasion plans. Mack, a sluggish and over-confident general, allowed himself to be surrounded at Ulm. Bavaria fell to the French, and Napoleon was soon in Vienna. Even when the Austrian and Russian armies made their expected junction, the sun of Austerlitz rose on the ruin of allied hopes. The parvenu Emperor had vanquished the old Empires.

Pitt had withstood the stress of Parliamentary debate unaided, amidst opposition criticism which was frequently peevish and invariably prejudiced, but the disgrace of Melville, accused of malversation of Admiralty funds in April 1805, had almost broken his nerve. The triumph at Trafalgar offset the disaster at Ulm, despite the grief occasioned by Nelson's death, and Pitt took fresh heart. In November, when he went to the Lord Mayor's banquet at the Mansion House, he was cheered in the streets, and in Cheapside the crowd untied the horses and dragged his carriage along themselves—a notable contrast to the jeers of the hungry 'nineties. At the dinner the Lord Mayor proposed Pitt's health as the saviour of Europe. His reply, the shortest and most felicitous of all his speeches, has become the most famous:

> I return you many thanks for the honour you have done me; but Europe is not to be saved by any single man. England has saved herself by her exertions, and will, as I trust, save Europe by her example.

He was on his feet for less than two minutes, but the impression made by his last public pronouncement was unforgettable. Over thirty years later the Duke of Wellington called it 'one of the best and neatest speeches I ever heard in my life'.

But Austerlitz shattered Pitt: all that he had worked for had crashed in confusion. His health cracked, and, whatever the truth in the story 'Roll up the map of Europe, it will not be needed these ten years', it reflects the tragic disillusionment of Pitt's last days. He now bore what Wilberforce uncannily called 'the Austerlitz look', and when he took the waters at Bath the crowd respectfully parted to let him pass. But the gout defied all that the doctors could do. Wracked by illness, Pitt sank into lassitude. After an agonising journey from Bath he reached his house at Putney on 11 January 1806. Lady Hester Stanhope was shocked at his emaciated appearance. He was sinking fast: interviews with old friends left him faint and exhausted. On 20 January he passed a bad night, and on the following morning he was clearly worse. He could take no nourishment, and on Wednesday, 22 January, he made his will. He was too weak to receive Holy Communion, but he prayed for a while with the Bishop of Lincoln:

> I have, as I fear is the case with many others, neglected prayer too much to allow me to hope that it can be very efficacious now. But I throw myself *entirely* upon the mercy of God through the merits of Jesus Christ.

With that boyish simplicity which he had never wholly lost he referred to the innocency of his life. The end was not far off.

His nephew, James Stanhope, watched by his bedside throughout that harrowing Wednesday and into the night. Pitt said good-bye to Lady Hester—'Dear soul, I know she loves me!'—and patiently endured his sufferings. When the doctor apologised for any pain he was causing him, he replied, 'I never take anything unkind that is meant for my good.' He became delirious, mumbling incoherently of the news from the East, and inquiring the direction of the wind. Even in the shadow of death he hoped that Prussian intervention would restore the fortunes of his country. From time to time he cried 'Hear! Hear!' as if in the Commons. Then he fell silent, the awful quiet being broken only by occasional moans. At midnight the rattles came into his throat. When a friend poured a little oil down his throat he gave a short, convulsive cough. But, suddenly, at half past two in the morning, he exclaimed, 'Oh, my country! How I leave my country!' For two hours more he lay still. At half past four in the morning his spirit passed peacefully and gently away. 'His life', Stanhope recalled, 'departed like a candle burning out.'

Pitt's death left the nation stunned and bewildered: Fox voiced the thoughts of all, when he remarked that it felt as if something was missing in the world. England's best-loved warrior and most famous statesman had been struck down within three months, and Charles Fox himself was to die before the year was out. At a time of unparalleled trial the great ones were vanishing from the earth. On the Continent Napoleon was triumphant. After Prussia was smashed at Jena, the settlement of Tilsit ushered in the most arrogant period of the French Empire. All that Pitt had most valued, all that he had died to preserve, was trampled in the dust beneath the conqueror's feet. Yet his spirit animated his successors. The lesser mortals stuck to their task with an obstinate courage which finally earned the proud reward of Waterloo. Only a few weeks before his death Pitt had predicted that Napoleon would be checked wherever he encountered the resistance of a people, and, with what Acton called the lucid prescience of his last days, named Spain as the place where this would be accomplished.

Castlereagh and Canning might dispute the right of succession, but after the death of Fox and the retirement of Grenville, most men thought of themselves as Pittites. His name became associated—however unjustly—with the toryism of the post-war years, and this has had grave consequences in the evaluation of his career. He left no school of statesmen, no organised party, and no body of doctrine. He bequeathed his memory to a handful of friends, and his example to his country. But, for a century and a half, his name has been bandied about in the eternal conflict between whig and tory. One detested him as an apostate; the other venerated him as a saint. Both were mistaken. Pitt was pre-eminently an eighteenth-century politician. His views of the place of the King in government, of party, of the Cabinet, of Parliamentary procedure, were all formulated in the 1780s and did not change. Even his strategy—in both its strength and weakness—looked back to the years when his father majestically controlled the nation's destinies. The idol of the tories called himself a whig. By reason of his dominance in the Cabinet, his long tenure of power, and his intellectual brilliance, he contributed to the development of the premiership, but he had no abstract conception of the office. When, in 1803, he insisted that there should be 'an avowed and real Minister, possessing the chief weight in the Council' he was thinking primarily of his working relationship with his colleagues. He was anxious to prevent a recurrence of the Loughborough episode, when a member of the Cabinet had used his position to undermine the King's confidence in his first minister. But this was a very different matter from imposing his will on the King, and to the end of his life Pitt respected the monarch's role in the executive government of the country. He accepted the conventions of his time, and plunged into the tasks of government. Despising pleas for pensions and ingratiating requests for place, he cold-bloodedly used the peerage as a convenient and inexpensive means of rewarding the faithful. He scorned the routine of party organisation, and had no party in the House, within the modern meaning of the term. His career makes sense only if it is seen in its eighteenth-century setting. To judge Pitt by twentieth-century political habits is to ignore the political structure within which he worked.

Yet liberal he was, in that he favoured reform. But his interest was that of the beneficent administrator, not the radical agitator. He was prepared to sacrifice theoretical consistency to the prospect of practical action. But the suggestion that he exploited the reform movement, only to drop it when it had served his purpose, is bizarre. Pitt's schemes of reform were frustrated by ignorance and prejudice, and by the political artifice of his opponents. The naïve assumption that resignation, or the threat of resignation, would have softened the hearts of hard-bitten eighteenth-century politicians, breaks down when confronted with the facts: Pitt's resignation in 1801 did not bring emancipation any nearer. The opposition to Parliamentary reform, to Catholic relief, to the abolition of the Slave Trade, to the reform of the Poor Law, to free trade with Ireland—all of these have been persistently underrated and misunderstood by whig historians. The miracle is that Pitt achieved so much.

The idea of Pitt as a cold, calculating, political machine is an old one. Coleridge expounded the thesis with all the inaccuracy of his genius in one of his *Morning Post* articles in 1800. Pitt was a man of words and abstractions, the prey of Customs House reports and Treasury statistics. Deprived of abstract phrases, he was reduced to impotent silence.

Indifferent to human feelings and natural beauty, he exulted in a sense of power, stimulating 'the glow of self-importance' by 'convivial indulgence'. There was some truth in what Coleridge said. Pitt was insensitive to music and neglected to patronise the arts. He could not understand the appeal of romantic idealism, or the irrational element in human affairs. But those who knew him best, remembered him as an affable companion, a man of gaiety and charm. He was generous to his mother and brother, when he could ill afford to be, and in his financial dealings he was scrupulously honest, although insolvent. His kindness to the Stanhope family earned him their undying gratitude, and when Lord Mahon married Lord Carrington's younger daughter, Pitt gave the newly weds a cottage at Walmer. He liked the company of children and young people. Reserved, aloof, and self-controlled, he was not inhuman. The price paid for fame—the unremitting toil, the desolate loneliness, the personal suffering—should not be left out of the reckoning.

The experience of two world wars, and the struggle against ideological totalitarianism, make possible a deeper understanding of the conflict with revolutionary France. Victorian liberals, secure in their assumption that freedom broadened down from precedent to precedent, and nurtured in the Foxite tradition so assiduously cultivated at Holland House, ignored the cataclysmic elements in both the French Revolution and Napoleon's career. Whilst resistance was branded as reaction Fox's record during the war years was deftly edited to sustain the myth that he was a disinterested, idealistic, liberal statesman. His ambition, inconsistency, and indifference to abstract political thinking, as well as his unpleasant aptitude for rejoicing at the reverses suffered by his own country, all dropped out of the picture. The most unreliable of English statesmen was credited with a cool dependability far removed from his passionate nature. The wayward, hot-headed Fox was cut down to size. Similarly, in their confident regard for Parliamentary institutions, they saw eighteenth-century politics in terms of Cabinet government, the premiership, and the two-party system. They were ill-informed on the day-to-day management of Parliamentary affairs, and ignorant of the social background to political life. They assumed that Pitt was a modern prime minister, supported in the Commons by a disciplined party. In their devotion to Fox they cast Pitt as the villain of the piece, or as a timorous reformer, scarcely worthy of the name. They praised

Fox as the forerunner of nineteenth-century liberalism: they failed to recognise Pitt's real—though limited—achievement.

Yet a curious uncertainty still shrouds his personality and place in history. His reputation has suffered both from hero-worship, which skimmed over the contradictions of his character, and from denigration, which was oblivious to its complexities. He remains an enigma, for his correspondence does not abound in those flashes of exuberant self-revelation which make Charles Fox and Edmund Burke so vivid and compelling. But the stabilisation of British economy after the American War, the reform of the customs, the pruning of wasteful expenditure, the restoration of national self-respect, and the courageous defence of English and European liberties threatened by an absolutism more powerful than the old, constitute an enduring claim to fame. Even an age made cynical by more recent wars of righteousness, and listless by the unceasing pursuit of affluence, can share the feelings of those Members of Parliament, who, on 7 May 1802, passed the resolution, 'That the Right Honourable William Pitt has rendered great and important services to his country, and especially deserves the gratitude of this House.' In that compliment, paid by his contemporaries when he was out of office, might be discerned the most eloquent tribute to his memory, and the surest testimony to his good name.

A NOTE ON FURTHER READING

THOSE who wish to follow up this short life of Pitt can easily be overwhelmed by an abundance of material. This selection of books is intended to open up the main topics touched upon in the present work, not to supply a comprehensive survey of the period. Many of the books listed are themselves only introductions to the further study of various aspects of Pitt's life and times, but perhaps they will be of some assistance to those who wish to explore more extensively for themselves.

There are two excellent general histories, both of which were recently published, Asa Briggs, *The Age of Improvement*, and J. Steven Watson, *The Reign of George III*. The latter contains a good bibliography. W. E. H. Lecky's classics, *A History of England in the Eighteenth Century* and *A History of Ireland in the Eighteenth Century*, remain the most rewarding accounts of the century as a whole, despite their limitations and anti-Pitt bias.

The fullest, and in many ways still the best, life of Pitt is that by Earl Stanhope, which contains a valuable selection of correspondence. This can be supplemented by J. Holland Rose's *William Pitt and National Revival* and the same author's *William Pitt and the Great War*, although these are excessively Pittite and rather ponderously written. Lord Rosebery's *Pitt* is a delightful book. D. G. Barnes's *George III and William Pitt, 1783–1806*, is a worth-while corrective to earlier accounts, but is marred by over-emphasis. There is some good reading in Holland

Rose's collection of essays, *Pitt and Napoleon*. The most readable life of Fox is that by Christopher Hobhouse, and although it is carelessly edited Lord John Russell's *Memorials and Correspondence of Charles James Fox* merits investigation. The two most approachable biographies of Burke are those by Sir Philip Magnus and Sir James Prior, but neither is as stimulating as T. W. Copeland's *Edmund Burke—Six Essays*. There is a lively account of George III in J. H. Plumb's *The First Four Georges*, which also presents a sympathetic portrait of the Prince of Wales. Sir Lewis Namier's essay on George III's character is printed in his *Personalities and Powers*. Richard Pares's *King George III and the Politicians*, is the best overall study of the constitutional problems of the reign. Economic history can be covered in two books by T. S. Ashton, *The Industrial Revolution*, in the Home University Library series, and *An Economic History of England: The Eighteenth Century*. British reactions to the French Revolution can be studied in A. Cobban's *The Debate on the French Revolution*, and in P. A. Brown's *The French Revolution in British History*. Fortunately both Burke's *Reflections on the French Revolution*, and Paine's *The Rights of Man*, are available in Everyman's Library. The attitudes of Pitt and Fox can be compared by reading *The War Speeches of William Pitt*, selected by R. Coupland, and the Everyman Library volume, *Fox's Speeches during the French Revolution*. Arthur Bryant has told the story of the wars against France in vivid style in *The Years of Endurance* and *The Years of Victory*, while Sir Julian Corbett's *The Campaign of Trafalgar*, puts the victory into perspective. Oliver Warner has written two attractive volumes, *The Battle of the Nile* and *Trafalgar*, both beautifully illustrated. The handiest introduction to the French Revolution is A. Goodwin's *The French Revolution*, Grey Arrow books, and this can be followed by the general histories by Madelin, J. M. Thompson, Mathiez, and Georges Lefebvre. Lord Acton's *Lectures on the French Revolution* are still worth reading, as is de Tocqueville's famous *L'Ancien Régime*. Two of the best lives of Napoleon are among the shortest: H. Butterfield's *Napoleon*, and H. A. L. Fisher's *Napoleon*.

For those interested in primary sources, the Pitt Papers are in the Public Record Office, and there are seventeen boxes of copies of his correspondence, from 1783, in the University Library, Cambridge.

Index